1995

The Decline of
American Political Parties
1952–1992

The Decline of
American Political Parties
1952–1992

Martin P. Wattenberg

Harvard University Press
Cambridge, Massachusetts, and London, England

This volume is an enlarged edition of *The Decline of American
Political Parties, 1952–1988,* published in 1990 by Harvard
University Press.

Library of Congress Cataloging-in-Publication Data

Wattenberg, Martin P., 1956–
   The decline of American political parties, 1952–1992 /
   Martin P. Wattenberg
     p. cm.
   Enl. ed. of: The decline of American political parties,
   1952–1988. 1990.
   Includes index.
   ISBN 0-674-19433-0
   1. Political parties—United States.   2. United States—Politics
and government—1945–1989.   3. United States—Politics and
government—1989–   I. Wattenberg, Martin P., 1956– Decline of
American political parties, 1952–1988.   II. Title.
JK2261.W37   1994   93-41952
324.273'09'045—dc20   CIP

For my parents

Contents

Preface, 1993

Over the four decades analyzed in this book, the American public has been drifting away from the two major political parties. Once central guiding forces in American electoral behavior, the parties are currently perceived with almost complete indifference by a large proportion of the population. Public affection for the parties has declined not because of greater negative feelings about the Democrats and Republicans, but rather because of an increasing sense that the parties are no longer crucial to the governmental process.

For example, 38 percent of the 1990 National Election Study respondents and 29 percent of those interviewed in the 1992 study gave the following responses to a series of four open-ended questions about the political parties:

Q. Is there anything in particular that you like about the Democratic Party?

A. No.

Q. Is there anything in particular that you dislike about the Democratic Party?

A. No.

Q. Is there anything in particular that you like about
    the Republican party?
A. No.

Q. Is there anything in particular that you dislike
    about the Republican party?
A. No.

When these questions were first asked in the 1952
election study, only 10 percent of the sample responded in this fashion. In Eisenhower and Kennedy's era,
such a response pattern typically reflected general
political ignorance. Most of these people had little to
say about the candidates either, and few voted. For
instance, 84 percent of the respondents with no opinion of the parties in the 1960 NES sample were classified as "no issue content" on Philip Converse's classic
measure of levels of conceptualization. In contrast,
only 44 percent of those who had nothing to say about
the parties failed to mention an issue when they were
asked about the candidates in 1984. In the 1980s and
1990s, such individuals tuned out the parties but
often not the candidates and the issues. Indeed, they
are often considered the most important group in
American electoral politics—"the floating voters."

It probably would have been better for the parties if
the public had become more negative rather than
more neutral toward them. Negative attitudes can easily be turned into positive attitudes by better performance or a change in policies. To induce people to
care about political parties once again may well be
more difficult. As I have argued in this book, it is
increasingly difficult for Americans to see the rele-

vance of political parties in this candidate-centered age of mass media.

The introduction and first eight chapters of this book make up the original study, outlining the evidence for party decline from 1952 to 1980 and the reasons for it. Chapter 9 addresses the central question of partisan attitudes in the 1980s, that of realignment. Although this chapter, covering the 1984 and 1988 elections, demonstrates a significant movement in favor of the Republicans, it reveals that partisanship in the electorate remained weak. Thus realignment was a hollow victory for the Republicans. Having more identifiers in the electorate is of greatly diminished value as long as many voters continue to split their tickets and focus their attention on individual candidates rather than on political parties.

The focus on candidates as opposed to parties was never so clear as in 1992. Ross Perot's independent candidacy illustrated that it is possible to completely ignore partisan labels and appeal directly to the public through the mass media. Chapter 10 analyzes the Perot vote, showing how the lack of support for either party opened the way for Perot to win the largest percentage of the vote of any independent candidate in the last eighty years. This chapter also addresses one of the most important by-products of party decline— the regular occurrence of divided party government in the United States.

Over the four editions of this book, I have been fortunate to have received much assistance from teachers, colleagues, and editors. I owe a special debt of gratitude to Philip Converse, Samuel Eldersveld, Arthur

Miller, and Warren Miller for steering me through the dissertation process at the University of Michigan, providing invaluable substantive and organizational advice. I also wish to thank several of my colleagues at the University of California, Irvine—Russ Dalton, Ami Glazer, and Bernie Grofman—for their helpful comments on Chapters 9 and 10. Over the past decade, Aida Donald and Elizabeth Suttell of Harvard University Press have smoothly guided the publication process. Countless improvements to the several editions of the book have been made by the Harvard University Press editors Katherine Brick, Ann Hawthorne, Elizabeth Hurwit, and Katarina Rice.

Introduction

Political parties have been accorded a preeminent position in the study of American politics. For nearly a century political scientists have written of the potential of political parties to establish effective popular control over the government. In a system designed to fragment political power, parties have been held to be the one institution capable of providing a unifying centripetal force. The functions that parties have been said to perform in American society are impressive and diverse. These include:

1. Generating symbols of identification and loyalty.
2. Aggregating and articulating political interests.
3. Mobilizing majorities in the electorate and in government.
4. Socializing voters and maintaining a popular following.
5. Organizing dissent and opposition.
6. Recruiting political leadership and seeking governmental offices.
7. Institutionalizing, channeling, and socializing conflict.

8. Overriding the dangers of sectionalism and promoting the national interest.
9. Implementing policy objectives.
10. Legitimizing decisions of government.
11. Fostering stability in government.

Given all of these functions, many political scientists have accepted E. E. Schattschneider's famous assertion that modern democracy is unthinkable save in terms of parties.[1] Not surprisingly, then, the various indications that political parties have weakened in recent years have been met with a great deal of alarm among commentators on American politics. David Broder, for example, has stated flatly, "The governmental system is not working because the political parties are not working."[2] Although most experts would not go so far, few would deny that the decline of American political parties has had a significant impact on the character of politics in this country.

Perhaps the most frequently cited consequences of the decline of parties are the growing importance of special interest groups and the dwindling of the principles of collective responsibility. The result, as Morris Fiorina has written, is that we now have "a system that articulates interests superbly but aggregates them poorly."[3] The making of public policy has thus become a more conflictual process with far less central direction and coherence. Individual policy decisions are increasingly made by ad hoc coalitions without relation to other policies. As Jimmy Carter found out during his four years in office, governing without the continuous support of a political party is an extremely difficult task.

Yet the question of party decline is a complex one, for political parties are complex, multifaceted institutions.

While most of the attention has been focused on the aspects of parties that have been weakened, there is evidence suggesting that in certain aspects parties have been strengthened. According to Malcolm Jewell and David Olson, for example, state political party organizations have been revitalized with the result being a more active role for state parties.[4] And on the national level, Cornelius Cotter and John Bibby have concluded from their extensive study of the history of national party organizations that there has been a growth in terms of institutionalization and nationalization of the parties in recent years.[5]

Thus, although most of the evidence does point toward party decline, to make global statements about the decay, decomposition, disappearance, or end of parties (as many have) may lead us to overlook the aspects of parties that have not been weakened. In order to get beyond the "sky-is-falling" stage in the discussion of parties, it must be recognized that not all the trends match and that evidence about one particular aspect is not necessarily generalizable to the condition of parties as a whole. As Austin Ranney has noted, those who have written about changes in the strength of parties all have something in mind, but the "something" differs from one observer to another.[6]

Political scientists who write about political parties fall into two main types, according to the noted British author S. E. Finer—"those who think of parties as things that *do*, and those who think of them as things that *are*."[7] The former primarily concern themselves with how well parties as organizations perform functions related to the machinery of government and the contesting of elections. Those among this school who are most empirically oriented study party activists and what they do; others study the various structures of the parties and how they operate. In contrast, writers who concern themselves with what parties are focus mainly on partisan attitudes among the mass public. Authors of this school address questions of alignment and dealignment in the party system, largely based on micro-level survey data on party identification and voting patterns.

This book clearly belongs in the latter category, but what political parties do has in fact been a prime motivating factor. If it were not for the crucial role that parties play in the operation of American government, the study of partisanship in the electorate would be far less important. Furthermore, one can reasonably infer that what parties are from the perspective of the mass electorate will have a major impact on what parties do in the political system. For example, if members of the electorate cast their ballots on the basis of factors other than partisanship, then those public officials who are elected can be expected to act more as individuals and less as members of a collective body committed to common goals. Similarly, if the mass public conceptualizes issues in terms of candidates rather than in terms of parties, then the direction of public policy can be expected to be hardly any more stable than the names on the ballot from year to year.

Of course, the flow of causality is by no means a unidirectional one from the state of parties in the electorate to the state of parties in government. If parties in government are weakened, the public will naturally have less of a stimulus to think of themselves politically in partisan terms. In fact, it will be argued here that one of the major factors behind the decline of partisanship in the electorate is that parties have become less integral in the processes of governing and campaigning, thereby resulting in the mass public's more neutral attitudes toward them. However, these altered public attitudes have themselves become a major reason why it will be very difficult to go back and reinstitutionalize political parties. Political behavior has a distinct habitual flavor to it—conceptualizing politics in a nonpartisan and candidate-centered fashion may well become a behavior pattern that could be difficult to alter.

The major objective of this book is to assess the extent of the decline of political partisanship in the electorate, the nature of the decline, and the reasons for it. The term "political partisanship" is a rather vague one, yet it is precisely because of this quality that I have chosen to use it, as it can be employed to refer to a broad range of public attitudes toward the parties. For too long research on the condition of parties in the electorate has concentrated almost solely on party identification. The research design employed here will emphasize using multiple methods to measure multiple traits of the public's attitudes toward the parties.

One limitation of the party identification scale is that one can only assess which party the respondent generally prefers and how strongly—it does not necessarily imply how positive, neutral, or negative people feel about the two parties. In order to understand what the distribution of party identification is likely to mean for the system, however, it is essential to know the evaluation nature of the attitudes on which it is based, that is, how each of the major alternatives are perceived. If we can ascertain what partisan preferences in the electorate represent about people's attitudes toward the parties, we will be much more likely to judge accurately what, if any, the long-term implications will be.

In addition to understanding the nature of the changes in the public's attitudes toward political parties, it is also important to know what has and what has not been an underlying cause of the changes which have occurred. If we want to know what, if anything, it will take to reverse the decline of partisanship in the electorate, we must first know what the sources of it have been. However, the causes of the decline are far less clear than the fact of the decline itself. Numerous possibilities have been discussed in the literature, but many are purely speculative and others leave key questions unanswered. A further shortcoming is that seldom has more than one explanation been considered and tested in the same analysis. Although not every conceivable factor can be examined here, a variety of possible factors will be explored, both for their theoretical significance and for their empirical plausibility.

This work is offered in the hope that it will add to our understanding of the American public's views of, and support for, the political parties. Because the study of party identification has contributed so heavily to what we know to date, it will be the major focus for the first few chapters. Next, other measures will be examined in order to provide a more in-depth understanding of the current state of political partisanship in the electorate and the nature of the changes that have taken place. Finally, the variables that may be responsible for the decline of partisanship will be examined.

1
The Concept of
Political Partisanship

"Despite there being a quite voluminous literature on partisanship as of the 1980s," Jack Dennis laments in a recent paper, "one looks in vain for any comprehensive statement of the theoretical meaning or purposes of the construct."[1] Perhaps the major reason for this shortcoming is that over the years many different scholars have used some variant of the concept for a wide variety of purposes. Furthermore, most of the working definitions of partisanship that have been employed have contained a high degree of construct validity. Thus, depending on the particular interests of the researcher, partisanship can take on numerous different theoretical meanings and purposes, thereby making it difficult for any single piece of research to treat the concept comprehensively. By devoting an entire book to the subject, it may be possible to at least partially overcome this difficulty.

Starting with the most practical purpose, partisanship can be used to predict voting behavior with a high degree of accuracy. Democrats tend to vote for Democratic candidates and Republicans tend to vote for Republican candidates. Such a pattern seemed so obvious to the

Columbia research group which conducted pioneering studies of voting in the 1940 and 1948 elections that they virtually ignored it.[2] Indeed, on the surface, to say that partisans usually vote for candidates from their own party seems tautological. If partisanship is no more than a reflection of voting intentions, why not address the question directly and just ask people how they will vote? Such a criticism has been the major focus of attention for many European scholars, who argue that because reports of party loyalty closely follow those of the vote, the concept of partisanship is not of much use in their countries.[3]

In the United States, however, one *can* clearly distinguish partisanship from voting behavior, as the correlation is far from perfect. What makes partisanship particularly interesting in the U.S. context, then, is not merely that it enables us to predict the vote, but also that it allows us to identify the situations in which voting behavior deviates from what we might normally expect. The fact that Jimmy Carter could have been expected to receive 55 percent of the two-party vote for president in 1980 based on the distribution of party identification in the electorate clearly does not reflect the election outcome very well, but it does give us a baseline from which to judge the magnitude of the candidate and issue factors that led to the Reagan victory.

In short, partisanship provides us with a means for distinguishing long-term from short-term change. Theoretically, its measurement taps a generalized standing decision on the part of the citizen to vote for a particular party under normal circumstances. Such a decision will of course not always be followed because circumstances are never completely "normal"; each election differs in many ways from the next in terms of the issues of the day and the candidates presented to the voters. However, because such factors influencing the vote usually last for only a short period of time, partisans are likely to return to the fold once such forces disappear from the political scene. A pattern in which individuals continue to be Democrats even though they voted for a particular Republican candidate (or vice versa) indicates that the shift in the vote is likely to be of short duration. In contrast, if the distribution of party loyalties also shifts, then what may seem to be a short-term change in the vote may in fact be an indication of a long-term change as well.

Such a theoretical framework for understanding voting behavior assumes that the distribution of partisanship in the electorate is more stable over time than election returns from year to year. This has undoubtedly been the case over the last three decades. Examining the presidential election returns from 1952 to 1980 leaves one with a distinct sense of the volatility of American electoral behavior. Except for the elections of 1952 and 1956, no two successive elections have produced anything approaching similar results. Close elections have alternated with landslides, and Democratic victories with Republican victories. In contrast, survey data from the Survey Research Center/Center for Political Studies (SRC/CPS) National Election Studies indicate a remarkable stability in the relative strength of the two parties nationwide in terms of psychological identification. Democrats have consistently outnumbered Republicans from 1952 to 1980 by an average ratio of approximately 1.7 to 1, which translates into an expected normal vote of roughly 54 percent Democratic when historical differences in turnout and defection rates are taken into account.[4] There has of course been some variation in this ratio over the years, but the standard deviation is only 1.7, compared to 7.0 for the actual vote. The stability of partisanship vis-à-vis the vote is also confirmed on the basis of individual-level panel data. For example, of the respondents in the 1972–1976 panel who voted in both presidential elections, 26 percent shifted their vote while only 7 percent changed their party affiliation from one party to the other.[5]

In sum, partisanship has been postulated in the political science literature as functioning as a preserving or stabilizing influence on public opinion, and consequently on the political system as well. According to Philip Converse and Georges Dupeux, the likelihood of voters' being attracted to "flash" parties and demagogic leaders is considerably lessened by the degree to which the citizens of a polity identify with one of the established parties.[6] It is naturally some sort of economic or cultural shock that leads to such sudden shifts of popular support, they write, but systems in which many voters do not have long-term partisan attachments are the most likely to be significantly affected.

The crucial assumption here is that partisanship represents a positive sense of affect toward one of the parties. This affect is often learned early in life from one's parents and theoretically grows stronger with age. What is most important is the psychological attachment involved, not any legal membership or contact with the party organization. Nevertheless, despite the stress on individual psychological dispositions, the group basis of partisanship was clearly central in the formulation of the well-known Michigan theory of party identification. As the authors of *The Voter Decides* wrote:

The present analysis of party identification is based on the assumption that the two parties serve as standard-setting groups for a significant proportion of the people of this country. In other words, it is assumed that many people associate themselves psychologically with one or the other of the parties, and that this identification has predictable relationships with their perceptions, evaluations and actions. These relationships would be expected to be in the areas of experience relevant to the activities of political parties.[7]

The emphasis on group attachment was further expanded upon by the Michigan scholars in The American Voter:

In characterizing the relation of individual to party as a psychological identification we invoke a concept that has played an important if somewhat varied role in psychological theories of the relation of individual to individual or of individual to group. We use the concept here to characterize the individual's affective orientation to an important group-object in his environment. Both reference group theory and small-group studies of influence have converged upon the attracting or repelling quality of the group as the generalized dimension most critical in defining the individual-group relationship, and it is this dimension that we call identification.[8]

Years later, Warren Miller noted that the term "identification" was "used quite intentionally to express the assumption that the relationship often involves an extension of ego." Generically, party identification is similar to religious identification: "In both instances the institution, that is the group, is concerned with defining the proper relationship between the person and the group-relevant components of social life. Indeed, the existence of the group, with acknowledged leaders who articulate the group's values and interpret the group's interest in the stream of public affairs, is crucial to the group member's ability to relate to the larger world."[9]

Party identification theoretically serves, then, as the primary source of *orientation* for an individual's political attitudes, just as religious denomination acts as an orientation for religious matters. Once one becomes psychologically attached to a party one tends to see political matters as other party members do. Being a Democrat therefore makes one more likely to give Democratic leaders the benefit of the doubt and to perceive issues in a Democratic light. Presumably, in many cases this is simply because of the identification itself rather than the result of a searching analysis of the candidates and current policy questions. (One of the key findings of the early Michigan voting studies was in fact the lack of political knowledge and involvement in the electorate.) In *The American Voter* such an effect of party identification was labeled a "perceptual screen"—through it one sees what is favorable to one's partisan orientation and filters out dissonant information. The stronger the party bond, the more likely the selection and distortion processes were found to be.

Partisanship thus plays a useful role for party leaders: it gives them a base of support in the electorate which can generally (within limits) be depended upon to view their actions in a favorable light. Just as the home team's fans will always tend to see the referee's close calls in favor of the home team, so will partisans support their party leaders in questionable cases.

The perceptual screening involved in party identification also facilitates the task of holding together the unusually diverse party coalitions that the American two-party system necessarily generates. Research has demonstrated that party identifiers adjust, or project, their perceptions of where the parties stand on issues in such a way that their own issue beliefs match those of their chosen party.[10] In other words, conservative Democrats will be more likely to see the Democratic Party as leaning toward conservative stands while liberal Democrats will be more likely to see the party as leaning in a liberal direction. The net result is to reduce the psychological issue distance between individuals and their respective parties, thereby giving party leaders room to maneuver within a limited issue space rather than tying them to fixed and uncompromisable positions.

In spite of these theoretical benefits to the political system, the process of perceptual screening involved in partisanship has often been interpreted by scholars as an indication that democracy in the United States is not functioning properly. If issue positions are merely the result of party identification, then what we may have is more of a *rationalizing* voter than a rational one, according to this line of thought. On the other hand, however, there clearly is a rationalistic aspect to party identification, which along with the group basis of the concept has received a good deal of attention in the literature. Electoral politics is inordinately more complicated and time-consuming for the average citizen in the United States than for those in almost any other democratic country in the world. First of all, Americans are expected to vote for a plethora of political offices including president, senator, representative, governor, state senator, state representative, mayor, city council members, school board members, sheriff, drain commissioner, and a host of others, depending on the locality. Second, American voters are asked to exercise their franchise unusually often. While the typical European voter may be called upon to cast two or three ballots in a four-year period, many Americans are faced with a dozen or more separate elections in the space of four years.[11]

To make a rough analogy, it would probably take an individual approximately the amount of time required for one or two college-level courses a year in order to cast a completely informed vote for all of these offices in all of these elections. Therefore, voters need shortcuts, or cues, such as partisanship to facilitate their decision-making. As Anthony Downs writes, "It may be rational for a man to delegate part or all of his political decision-making to others, no matter how important it is that he make correct decisions."[12] Given that the two parties do consistently offer fairly distinctive (if not diametrically opposing) alternatives, delegating one's vote along party lines tends to facilitate representation even though one may know absolutely nothing about the particular issue stands of the candidates who are on the ballot.[13]

Those who stress the rational basis of party identification usually concentrate on the cognitive side of partisanship rather than on the affective link emphasized in *The American Voter*. Such analysts construe party loyalties as largely a reflection of people's evaluations of the past and current performance of the two parties. For example, Fiorina defines party identification as "the difference between an individual's past political experiences with the two parties ... Past political experiences, of course, are simply the voters subjectively weighted retrospective evaluations formed while observing the postures and performances of the contending parties during previous election periods."[14] Within such a framework, partisanship is both an exogenous and an endogenous variable. In other words, not only will one's identification affect how one views political issues and leaders, but so also will the short-term forces affect party identification. Making use of the available panel data on party identification, some scholars have concluded that variation over time on the individual level, far from being random noise, follows predictable patterns on the basis of recent party fortunes, new issues, or changes in existing issue preferences.[15] As Charles Franklin and John Jackson write, "In this way, each campaign leaves its imprint, or residue, on individual identifications."[16] Thus, from a cognitive psychological perspective, partisanship can be postulated as serving as an economizing or storage device, enabling the individual to keep a running scorecard on the performance of the two parties in order to guide his or her voting decisions.

Finally, partisanship has also been viewed as encompassing a variety of normative attitudes regarding the role that political parties should play in the American governmental system. The formal theory for this view has best been expressed by Herbert Weisberg, who argues that party identification should be viewed as a multidimensional concept that taps separate attitudes toward the Democratic and Republican parties, political independence, and political parties in general.[17] In short, partisanship may stand for support for the *institution* of the political party as well as support for a particular party.

Data from the 1980 national election study make it possible to test such an assumption on a nationwide scale thoroughly for the first time. As Table 1.1 shows, party identifiers were far more likely than nonpartisans to express support for a variety of aspects concerning political parties as institutions. Weak partisanship and espe-

Table 1.1 Normative attitudes toward political parties

	Strong partisans	Weak partisans	Non-partisans[a]
The truth is, we probably don't need political parties in America anymore.			
Agree	20.9	30.2	42.6
Pro-con	6.3	13.0	13.3
Disagree	72.8	56.8	44.1
It would be better if in all elections we put no party labels on the ballot.			
Agree	33.9	44.8	59.8
Pro-con	9.0	14.7	36.5
Disagree	57.1	36.5	27.6
The parties do more to confuse the issues than to provide a clear choice on the issues.			
Agree	46.0	56.6	62.2
Pro-con	16.1	24.2	20.1
Disagree	37.9	19.2	17.7
It is better to be a firm party supporter than to be a political independent.			
Agree	61.6	32.5	10.9
Pro-con	15.5	15.9	9.8
Disagree	22.9	51.6	79.2
The best rule in voting is to pick a candidate regardless of party label.			
Agree	58.6	74.2	82.9
Pro-con	9.2	9.9	5.6
Disagree	32.3	15.9	11.4

a. Independent leaners are combined here with pure Independents, as no significant differences were found on any of these questions.
SOURCE: 1980 CPS National Election Study.

cially independence are associated with feelings that parties are unnecessary in our system, that they do more to confuse than to clarify issues, and that one should vote for the man and not the party. It is interesting to note, however, that such attitudes are quite widespread even among strong partisans. For example, more of these respondents agreed than disagreed with the statements that parties confuse the issues and that the best rule in voting is to pick a candidate regardless of party label. Patterns such as these have prompted Jack Dennis to write that "we may be called upon in the not so distant future to witness the demise of a once prominent institution of American government and politics,"[18] that is, the political party.

Americans have always tended to view parties rather ambivalently, however, beginning with the Founding Fathers.[19] Thus in order to make even a preliminary assessment of assertions of the demise of partisanship in the electorate, the empirical evidence over time must be carefully examined. Two well-known classes of evidence will be looked at—one concerning the changing relationship of party to the vote and the other dealing with the frequency and strength of party identification over time.

The Decline of Party Voting

Although sample survey evidence is necessarily limited to the relatively recent period for which data are available, one can take a far more extended historical perspective on partisanship and its relation to the vote by examining aggregate election returns over time. We would expect that if party loyalties are closely related to the vote, the results for different offices in the same election should closely parallel one another. Therefore, if a Democratic candidate wins the race in a given district for president, then other Democratic candidates in the district should also win. If, however, voters are casting their ballots on the basis of factors other than party, ticket-splitting may result in victories for some candidates on the ticket and losses for others. Such a phenomenon has been termed "electoral disaggregation" by Walter Dean Burnham, whose *Critical Elections and the Mainsprings of American Politics* offers one of the most comprehensive treatments of aggregate historical voting patterns.[20]

Perhaps the most often quoted statistic that Burnham uses to demonstrate the growth of electoral disaggregation is the percentage of districts in which there is a split in the outcome for the presidential versus the congressional race. Because the unit of analysis is identical from election to election and every part of the country can be incorporated in the analysis, such a measure seems to be reasonably consistent over time and capable of tapping national trends. As Figure 1.1 shows, the proportion of split results has risen quite markedly over the last sixty years. Only about 10 to 15 percent of the 435 congressional districts had split results in the 1920–1944 period. In the twenty years between 1944 and 1964, however, this figure gradually rose to about 30 percent. And in 1972 one finds an all-time high of 44 percent, which indicates that the occurrence of an identical outcome for both races was hardly any greater than would be expected by chance.

Of course these data are subject to aggregate fallacy: one could theoretically find many people splitting their tickets in a district where the outcome in both races is nevertheless similar, or alternatively one could find a split result caused by only a few people crossing party lines.[21] However, the data do provide an indication that the decline in straight-ticket voting may have begun before the first SRC national election study in 1952. Furthermore, such a pattern almost certainly rules out the possibility that any increase in split-ticket voting found subsequent

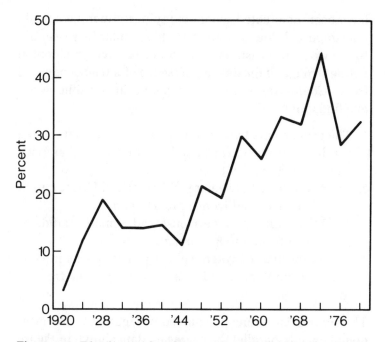

Figure 1.1   Districts with split presidential and House results, 1920–1980

Sources: Data for 1920–1976 taken from John F. Bibby, Thomas E. Mann, and Norman J. Ornstein, *Vital Statistics on Congress, 1980* (Washington, D.C.: American Enterprise Institute, 1980); 1980 data calculated by the author from election returns.

to the early election studies is merely a return to normalcy.

Examining the individual-level survey data from the period between 1952 and 1980 confirms the conclusion from the aggregate statistics that the degree of electoral disaggregation has risen quite sharply over the last few decades. As Warren Miller and Teresa Levitan have rightly argued, one possible reason for the increase in ticket-splitting is simply that specific presidential candidates have been nominated whom many party members could not support.[22] However, the fact that secular increases are found even in measures that do not involve presidential voting strongly indicates the presence of a true behavioral trend. Comparing the two end points in the time series one finds that:

1. The proportion of voters reporting that they have voted for different parties in presidential elections has risen from 29 to 57 percent.
2. Ticket-splitting between presidential and House candidates has increased from 12 to 34 percent.
3. Ticket-splitting between House and Senate candidates has grown from 9 to 31 percent.
4. The proportion of voters splitting their tickets in elections for other state and local offices has gone from 27 to 59 percent.

The survey data trends displayed in Figure 1.2, however, do not exactly parallel the aggregate data shown in Figure 1.1. Despite the change between 1952 and 1960 in the proportion of split results on the district level, the individual-level data indicate very little change during this period. Conversely, after 1964 the aggregate data appear fairly stable, except for the short-lived increase in 1972; the individual-level data, on the other hand, show a continued steady increase on all four measures through 1980.

The contrasts between the survey evidence and the aggregate voting patterns suggest caution in interpreting even major across-the-board gains for one party as necessarily indicating a resurgence of partisanship. For example, the fact that Ronald Reagan's victory in 1980, unlike that of Richard Nixon's in 1972, was accompanied by large gains for the Republicans in both the House and the

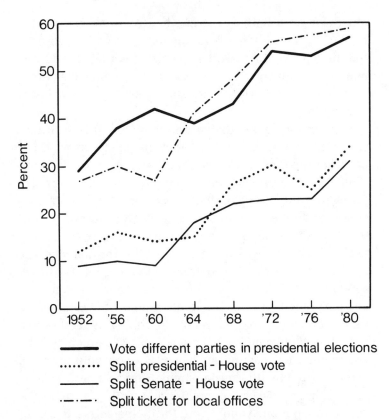

Figure 1.2 Trends in split-ticket voting, 1952–1980
Source: SRC/CPS National Election Studies.

Senate has led many to speculate that the era of ticket-splitting may be coming to an end. Even the noted Democratic pollster Patrick Caddell, whose political position might predispose him toward alternative explanations for his party's congressional losses in 1980, has noted the apparent return of coattail voting. "A continuation of this trend," writes Caddell, "could be a positive development for both parties, and an opportunity for one or the other—or even both—to strengthen its weak grip on the public."[23] Yet it is clear from the data shown in Figure 1.2 that the apparent rise in straight-ticket voting in 1980 was merely an optical illusion, and that on the behavioral level the parties' grip on the electorate in fact reached a new all-time low.

Furthermore, given the current state of public attitudes concerning party-line voting, there is good reason to expect that the process of electoral disaggregation may continue for some time to come. The attitudinal potential for ticket-splitting has consistently been greater than its incidence, and as such one can reasonably interpret recent trends as reflecting the tendency for behaviors eventually to come into line with attitudes. In 1952, for instance, the SRC election study posed the following question to respondents: "Some people think that if a voter votes for one party for President he should vote for the same party for Senator and Congressman. Do you agree or disagree with this statement?" Although over 80 percent of the voters reported casting such a party-line vote, only 40 percent agreed with the statement. Similarly, Jack Dennis reports that a 1956 Gallup poll found that 74 percent of the public thought one should vote for the person rather than the party; in 1968 the figure was 84 percent.[24] And finally, in the 1980 election study respondents were asked to agree or disagree on a seven-point scale with the statement, "The best rule in voting is to pick a candidate regardless of party label." The results reveal not only that such a view is widely held, but also that it is held with great intensity by many:

Disagree						*Agree*
1	2	3	4	5	6	7
9%	4%	5%	8%	11%	21%	41%

To recapitulate, it is clear that partisanship has declined substantially from the perspective of its ability to structure the vote. Ticket-splitting has assumed massive proportions compared to the rate just two decades ago, and only a small minority of the electorate now believes that one should vote strictly on the basis of party labels.

The Decline of Party Identification

Accompanying the trend toward greater split-ticket voting there has also been a decline in party identification. Election studies during the period from 1952 to 1964 consistently found that approximately 75 percent of the electorate identified themselves as either Democrats or Republicans, and roughly half of these identifiers considered themselves to be strong partisans. The similarity in the party identification marginals from one sample survey to another during this period led Philip Converse to write of the "serene stability in the distribution of party loyalties" expressed by the public,[25] and later to call these years the "steady state period" with regard to party identification.[26] Figure 1.3 shows that after 1964 the picture changed somewhat, however. Between 1964 and 1972 the percentage of respondents identifying with one of the two major parties declined from 77 to 64 percent. In addition, people who continued to identify with a party after 1964 expressed a weaker sense of identification than previously. Although strong partisans were almost as numerous as weak partisans from 1952 to 1964, by 1972 the latter outnumbered the former by a ratio of slightly over three to two.

At first, these changes in the distribution of party loyalties were seen as quite a revolutionary development. For example, Burnham wrote that the losses in identification

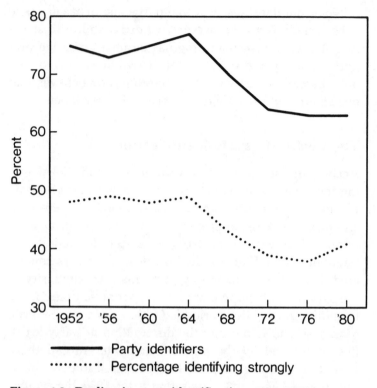

Figure 1.3 Decline in party identification, 1952–1980
Source: SRC/CPS National Election Studies.

for both parties could very well represent "a dissolution of the parties as action intermediaries in electoral choice and other politically relevant acts." In addition, the rise of a "mass base for independent political movements of ideological tone and considerable long-term staying power" seemed to be one possible consequence of the decline, according to Burnham.[27] Similarly, Gerald Pomper wrote that the continuation of such a trend "may eventually bring the nation to a free-floating politics, in which prediction is hazardous, continuities are absent, and governmental responsibility is impossible to fix."[28] In Pomper's view, the implications for democracy seemed quite threatening.

More recently, however, a revisionist view has come into prominence; it perceives the decline in party identification as far less cataclysmic. To begin with, the downward trend no longer seems to be a trend at all, but rather a limited period effect in which there was a rapid decline followed by the development of a new level of stability. Furthermore, the period of weakening party loyalties— 1964 to 1972—was clearly an unusually tumultuous epoch in the history of American politics, which may well never again be duplicated in the severity of the shocks (Vietnam, racial unrest, and so on) felt by the electorate.[29]

Perhaps more important is the analytic argument by Bruce Keith et al. that the decline in party identification has been vastly exaggerated by considering as nonpartisans Independents who report that they think of themselves as closer to one of the two parties.[30] These so-called "Independent leaners" are not an uncommitted and unmobilized bloc, according to these scholars, but are instead largely "closet" Democrats and Republicans. Although they may prefer to call themselves Independents than Democrats or Republicans, when it comes to their voting behavior in presidential elections they tend to act just as partisan as weak party identifiers. Between 1952 and 1980 the mean defection rate for weak Democrats was 35 percent, compared to 34 percent for Independent Democrats; likewise, weak Republicans defected 16 percent of the time on the average, compared to 15 percent for Independent Republicans.[31] If one therefore considers Independent leaners as simply partisans by another name, then the proportion of the population identifying with a party can hardly be said to have declined at all over the years. As Keith et al. write, "Most of the growth in Independents has occurred among the hidden partisans, while the high-level speculations have concerned the genuine Independents, whose increase has been rather modest."[32]

From a somewhat different perspective, Philip Converse and Gregory Markus have also made a major contribution to the school of thought which argues that the erosion of partisan ties has not been as sharp as people such as Burnham or Pomper would have us believe.[33] One of the most important early findings concerning the concept of party identification was that the stability in individual placement on the scale far exceeded the stability of any other attitudinal variable in the 1956–1960 election study panel. Such a pattern led Converse to conclude that party identification was clearly the most central attitude in the mass public's political belief system.[34]

Subsequent writings that argued the case for the destabilization of party identification, however, did so without the benefit of more recent panel data in order to test whether party loyalties had in fact become more volatile. The conclusion seemed logical, given the changes that had occurred since the 1950s, but yet it remained purely speculative. It was not until the completion of a second long-term panel study, undertaken between 1972 and 1976, that a direct test of the proposition became possible. And as Converse and Markus reported, the massive change that might have been expected was not at all confirmed. The average two-year continuity correlation for party identification was found to be .813 in this later period compared to .835 during the 1956–1960 period. Therefore, despite the fact that strength of party identification has declined somewhat, Converse and Markus conclude that it continues to be the most stable object of political orientation, followed by evaluations of major presidential candidates and issue positions.[35]

Taking into account all of the recent revisionist points concerning the decline of party identification, it appears that the rise of split-ticket voting has been a much sharper and long-lasting trend. Therefore, it follows logically that a good portion of the increase in electoral disaggregation has been due to partisans' using their identifications less and less as a cue in voting behavior.[36] One possible explanation for such a pattern is that perhaps party identification simply means less to people across all levels than in the past. That is, continued identification with a party may not necessarily imply a continued high degree of importance for the identification.

The major problem with such an interpretation, of course, is Converse and Markus's argument that party identification remains the most *stable* political attitude among the mass public, with hardly any visible sign of a decline at all in this respect. But does stability necessarily indicate centrality? Certainly the reverse is true—that is, instability points to a lack of centrality—but there is no reason to believe that stability is by itself *prima facie* evidence for centrality. The fact that party identification has declined in its importance as a shaper of thought and determiner of opinion implies that the centrality of the labels of Democrat, Independent, and Republican may be far less than one might be led to believe by their across-time stability. In the next chapter we shall examine the stability question in greater detail by broadening the analysis to other pieces of data about public attitudes toward the parties, all of which call into question whether partisan attitudes are in fact uniquely central to the electorate.

2
The Stability of Partisan Attitudes

Despite the great reliability associated with the measurement of party identification, there has of late been a flurry of research activity criticizing the construct validity of the traditional seven-point scale. Specifically, it has been argued that the unidimensionality implicit in the construction of the scale is inappropriate because it assumes that partisanship and independence are mutually exclusive alternatives and that an individual must be one or the other.[1] These scholars maintain that party identification should be viewed as a multidimensional concept that involves components of partisan direction and strength *as well as a nonpartisanship component.*

For our purposes, the multidimensionality of party identification is particularly relevant because it raises questions about which dimension, or dimensions, of the scale account for its reliability. Is the high continuity correlation for the party identification measure due mostly to the stability of evaluative attitudes about the two parties or to attitudes of nonpartisanship? Only the former can be used as even inferential evidence for the centrality of party over other political attitudes.

From the early writings on independence, the concept of nonpartisanship was established in the discipline as a rather unstable attitude. For example, in an article devoted to the measurement and characteristics of independence, Samuel Eldersveld described Independents as "the segment of the electorate which is highly irregular in party allegiance."[2] Contrary to the normative ideal of the Independent as one who carefully weighs the appeals of both parties on the basis of all the available information, they were invariably found to be less informed about, and involved in, politics than party identifiers. As Campbell et al. stated, "The individual who has a strong and continuing involvement in politics is likely to develop a commitment to one or the other of the major parties."[3]

Under this framework, nonpartisanship was considered as quite often just a temporary phase one might go through before settling with one of the parties as one's "standing decision." However, it is one of the key points of this book that as political parties have become less salient to the electorate, a lack of party identification has increasingly come to represent a sense of *indifference* toward both the Democrats and the Republicans. Thus, given that Independents are relatively unconcerned with political parties, their nonpartisanship may be just as stable as the partisanship of Democratic and Republican identifiers. Such a hypothesis is in fact nicely confirmed by data from the 1980 election study panel, in which all respondents were asked separately whether they considered themselves a supporter of one of the political parties and whether they ever thought of themselves as a political independent. Between January and September 78 percent responded identically to the party support question compared to 75 percent on the question of political independence.

Thus the party identification scale is probably not entirely appropriate to measure whether evaluations of political parties are the most central of all political orientations. The stability of nonpartisanship indicates the lack of centrality of parties for the respondent, yet it contributes to a correlation that has been widely interpreted as demonstrating the continued importance of partisan attitudes. Therefore, we shall turn to more direct measures of evaluations of each of the two parties in order to test whether such an interpretation is in fact warranted.

Feeling Thermometer Ratings of the Parties

One particularly useful methodological device for comparing the stability of evaluations of a variety of political objects is the feeling thermometer. Through the use of the standardized zero-to-one-hundred scale, comparability problems in question wording are greatly reduced. One does not have to worry whether the possible alternatives in the question are worded better than in another—only whether the stimuli ("Democrats," "Liberals," and so on) are phrased sensibly.

Converse and Markus have examined the stability of thermometer ratings of presidential candidates in the 1972–1976 panel and found that the continuity correlations for candidates fall significantly below the correlation for party identification. However, when one examines ratings of "Democrats" and "Republicans," the continuity correlations are actually somewhat *lower* than those for most leaders:

Ted Kennedy	.67	*Democrats*	.47
George Wallace	.62	Richard Nixon	.45
George McGovern	.54	*Republicans*	.43
Hubert Humphrey	.53	Henry Jackson	.34

Thus, by squaring the correlations, we find that ratings of Ted Kennedy between 1972 and 1976 shared 45 percent common variance compared to only 22 percent for ratings of "Democrats."

One possible problem with such a finding is that the wording of "Democrats" and "Republicans" is a bit ambiguous. Respondents might quite reasonably personalize the referent to include friends and neighbors as well as specific party leaders. Fortunately, one can assess the stability of ratings of the Democratic and Republican *parties* based on collection of panel data in January and September of 1980. These data show a slightly better picture for the stability of partisan attitudes, but again one finds that the continuity correlations are not any higher than for evaluations of political leaders:

Ted Kennedy	.69	Ronald Reagan	.54
Democratic Party	.65	*Republican Party*	.54
Gerald Ford	.63	Walter Mondale	.52
Jimmy Carter	.61	Jerry Brown	.49
George Wallace	.60	Howard Baker	.44
George McGovern	.59	George Bush	.39
John Connally	.58		

Clearly, the interpretation indicated by the feeling thermometer data is that although party identification is a uniquely stable attitudinal variable, evaluations of political parties are not. One reason why party identification is so stable over time is undoubtedly that unlike most other attitudinal variables it involves a process of self-labeling. However, the fact that party evaluations are no more stable than candidate evaluations implies that these labels are not as salient to individual respondents as one might infer from the high degree of reliability associated with them. It has often been argued that although the reliability of public responses to issue questions is extremely low, the underlying opinions are nevertheless quite stable.[4] In this case just the reverse seems true—the responses are far more stable than the underlying attitudes that they supposedly represent.

The question that this finding naturally raises is whether such has always been the case or whether the stability of evaluations of the parties has in fact declined over time. In order to investigate this question we need to compare the stability of evaluations of the parties in the 1956–1960 panel to that in the 1972–1976 panel.

Decline in the Stability of Party Evaluations over Time

Unfortunately, the 1956–1960 panel was conducted before the introduction of the feeling thermometer into the election studies, so it is impossible to determine whether the stability of these ratings has declined over the years. However, both the 1956–1960 panel and the 1972–1976 panel contain identical open-ended questions that ask respondents what they like and dislike about each of the two parties. By counting the number of likes and then subtracting the number of dislikes, one can create summary scores that represent respondents' evaluations of the two parties.[5]

As hypothesized, the results show that on these measures the continuity correlations have fallen over time. In the 1956–1960 panel the continuity correlation for evaluations of the Democratic Party was .51; by the 1972–1976 panel this figure had fallen to .41. Similarly, for evaluations of the Republican Party one finds a decline in stability from .50 in the early panel study to .39 in the more recent study. Finally, in order to more closely approximate the bipolar nature of the party identification scale it is possible to create a party-affect scale by constructing a difference measure between each respondent's evaluations of the two parties. This measure yields somewhat higher correlations within each panel but again shows a decline over time—from .61 in 1956–1960 to .50 in 1972–1976.

Although these changes may not seem to be much on the surface, if one examines the percentage of variance explained, the decline in the stability of party evaluations is between 30 and 40 percent in the space of a decade and a half. Such a trend, furthermore, is more than just a reflection of the decline in strength of party identification. It is true that in both panels the stronger one's party identification the more likely one is to evaluate the parties consistently over time. However, except in the case of pure Independents, each level of strength of party identification shows a substantial decline in stability of party evaluations from the 1950s to the 1970s.

Generational replacement and the lowering of the voting age also do not provide much of an explanation. Given the fact that older people evaluate the parties with more stability than younger respondents, one might, under normal circumstances, expect to find that as age cohorts pass through the life-cycle the consistency of their evaluations should increase. In the period between the two long-term panels, however, just the opposite trend is found to have occurred within each cohort.

This is not to say that the decline in strength of party identification and the influx of young voters has not had an effect on the overall stability of party evaluations by the electorate. Both trends have indeed increased the proportion of people whom we would expect to have the least stable evaluations. However, the important point to note is that the greater instability in party evaluations is independent of each, and therefore indicative of a previously unrecognized change in the nature of public attitudes toward the political parties.

The results of this chapter lead us to question the esteemed position of partisan attitudes in the literature on voting behavior. Upon closer scrutiny it has been found that political parties are not the most stable objects of political orientation after all; both partisans and nonpartisans no longer evaluate the parties as consistently as they did in the past. Party identification may be just as stable overall as it was two decades ago, but nevertheless political parties no longer mean as much to people as they once did, as evidenced by the decline in the stability of party evaluations. What the growth in the popularity of the label "Independent" means has not been very well established, however. That will be the major task of the next chapter.

3
Independent or No Preference?

Political independence has probably been the most intensely scrutinized and debated aspect of the concept of party identification. Although the partisan balance has remained relatively stable for decades, the proportion of Americans known as "Independents" has risen substantially since the mid-1960s. Because citizens who do not identify with a political party are generally seen as holding the balance of power, such an increase is both strategically significant for those concerned with winning elections and theoretically significant for scholars concerned with the stability of the American party system. Much academic discussion has centered on the generational makeup of this group,[1] their political sophistication,[2] and the possibility that many may in fact be "closet partisans."[3]

Throughout all of this controversy and debate, however, one central and substantively relevant methodological point has been largely ignored—namely, that a respondent does not necessarily have to say that he or she is an Independent to be classified as such. Virtually all of the research that has been done using the standard measure of party identification has employed the derived scale without any analysis of the different paths by which it is possible to reach the same point on the scale. Yet, as Philip Converse has written, there is a small but significant fraction of the American population to whom "the notion of an abiding loyalty to a political party which underlies the party identification measure is next to meaningless. When posed the party identification question in an interview situation, many of this remnant give responses which properly get them coded as 'apolitical' or, as is a bit more misleading, as 'Independents.' "[4]

It is the central argument of this chapter that the "remnant" Converse describes is no longer just a remnant. In fact, the growth of this group in recent years accounts for most of the increase in the Independent categories on the party identification scale. Such a trend, however, is not an indication of an increase in the proportion of traditional apoliticals, who have virtually no interest in politics, but rather is yet another indication of the declining importance of political parties in the eyes of the American public.

Perhaps the most fundamental premise of the concept of independence is that there is something which one is independent *from*. In the case of political independence this is of course the political parties. It is one of the key hypotheses of this study, however, that political parties have been becoming increasingly meaningless to the electorate since the early 1950s. Thus the question of either identifying with one of the parties or being independent from both may be considerably less relevant to respondents than in the past and therefore much more likely to draw the simple answer "I don't have any preference at all." The difference between this response and saying

"I'm an Independent" may seem to be a subtle one, given that both represent a lack of partisanship, but the interpretation of party decline in the electorate is quite different when one takes into account the fact that the former type of response has been increasing far more rapidly than the latter. Instead of representing a conscious decision on the part of many to disdain from partisan labels, such a finding suggests that the decline of party identification has more likely resulted from a decrease in the salience of parties as attitudinal objects in the United States. What we are thus witnessing is the rise of a type of nonpartisan that the party identification scale cannot distinguish—one who is somewhat aware of political matters but lacks responsiveness to the concepts of either partisanship or independence.

The Increase in "No Preference"

The lead question in the party identification sequence is perhaps the best known in the history of survey research. If there were a Hall of Fame for mass survey questions, there is no doubt that "Generally speaking, do you usually consider yourself a Democrat, a Republican, an Independent, or what?" would be enshrined in it. Yet coding the responses to the question is not as simple as one might expect from its closed-ended nature, for not everyone chooses one of the three categories enumerated in the question. Many respond in such a way that they are initially coded as having no preference, given that they don't consider any of the labels in the question as applicable to them. A few examples from the interview protocols (some of which are quite common, others of which are obviously idiosyncratic) will help illustrate the type of responses frequently obtained from these individuals:

"Nothing in that respect. I don't consider myself anything politically."

"I ain't none of them."

"None."

"Not anything."

[Laughs.] "You should call me nothing."

"No preference."

"I don't think of myself as anything."

"It depends."

"I'm an American [citizen]."

"Oh hell, I don't know."

"May the best man win. It's the best candidate."

[Interviewer asks if respondent would call himself an Independent.] "You don't mean one of those minority groups?"

"I'm a person who believes in what I believe is a good man who will do the most for the country."

[Interviewer repeats question.] "I'm not a Republican, not a Democrat, not an Independent, and not a Communist."

"I'm nothing. I don't holler about it."

These comments suggest that the party identification question lacked substantive meaning for these people and that none of the choices offered was seen by them as a relevant political reference point. Yet each of these respondents was eventually coded as an Independent on the party identification scale.

How do such people end up as Independents even though they fail to identify themselves as such? In the case of those who are categorized as pure Independents, the decision is based on the respondent's interest in politics. Respondents are classified as apoliticals *only* if they (1) express no preference to the initial party identification question; (2) say that they do not lean toward either party; and (3) show little interest in politics. If after meeting the first two criteria the respondent shows interest in politics, he or she is moved *by the election study staff* to the pure Independent slot on the scale; the apolitical classification is reserved only for those who are almost totally uninterested and uninformed about politics.

Through 1964 such judgments by the election study staff were made largely on the basis of how the respondents reacted to the question, as there was a full line on the interview schedule to record each individual's answer. After 1964 the format of the interview protocol was changed slightly by printing boxes for the interviewer to check ("Democrat," "Republican," "Independent," "no preference," "other party"). Beginning in 1966, therefore, the interviewers could simply check the "no preference" box without recording the actual response, which made it necessary for the study staff to skim through the rest of the protocol to determine whether the person was interested in politics or not.[5]

In the case of those who indicate a lack of any preference on the initial question but who state that they lean toward one of the two parties, the coding has always been a clear-cut procedure. These people are automatically classified as Independent leaners despite the fact that *they have not identified themselves* as Independents. Yet many in this group really do not consider themselves as anything politically and merely pick a partisan leaning under the pressure of the interview situation. In one example of this phenomenon, a respondent in the 1964 study answered "I don't know" to the lead party identification question and then, in response to the question of whether she leaned toward either party, asked the interviewer which party Johnson represented and which Goldwater was from. When the interviewer explained the situation (contrary to accepted interviewing procedures), the respondent then said that she leaned toward the Democrats. Such a response, rather than revealing a long-term psychological disposition, clearly has more to do with the respondent's short-term intentions.

In all, there are five categories of nonpartisans to be examined. First, there are the traditional apoliticals for whom the party identification question has little meaning and who simply are not at all interested in politics. Then there are the two groups who are not classified as apoliticals but who express no preference to the lead question—one of these groups leans toward neither party and the other group does indicate a partisan leaning. Finally, there are the two groups of people who actually identify themselves as Independents—nonleaners and leaners.[6]

Table 3.1 shows the proportion of the population in each of these five categories in presidential election years from 1964 to 1980, the period heralded as that of the rise of independence.[7] The data show that the increase in self-classified Independents was quite real between 1964 and 1968. In both years the two no-preference categories were quite negligible, representing less than 10 percent of all those classified as Independents on the party identification scale. However, between 1968 and 1976 the proportion of self-classified or "real" Independents increased very little, and the 1980 figures show a clear decline to below the comparable 1968 levels. In contrast, the two no-preference categories have increased steadily since 1968 to the point where they now combine to represent nearly 10 percent of the population and 30 percent of the Independents on the scale as traditionally derived.[8] When

Table 3.1 Trends in the proportions of nonpartisan groups

Year	Apoliticals	No-preference neither	No-preference leaner	Independent neither	Independent leaner
1964	0.9	1.1	1.0	6.7	13.9
1968	1.4	1.2	1.3	9.3	17.2
1972	1.4	3.7	2.6	9.4	18.6
1976	0.9	4.4	2.6	10.0	18.6
1980	2.2	5.2	4.5	7.7	16.7

SOURCE: SRC/CPS National Election Studies.

these respondents are removed from the Independent category, we find the self-labeled Independents are hardly any more numerous now than during the era that Converse has labeled as the steady-state period of strength of partisanship.

Are They Apoliticals?

The major question that this finding raises is whether citizens in the two no-preference categories should in fact be considered apoliticals rather than Independents. Table 3.2 shows that on a variety of measures of political involvement, based on pooled data from the 1964, 1968, 1972, 1976, and 1980 studies,[9] they are not strictly one or the other. Compared to the respondents who have always been classified as apoliticals, they vote more frequently, have greater interest in the campaign, and have a higher level of subjective political competence or internal efficacy. Thus they are hardly so far removed from politics as to be rightly considered apolitical. On the other hand, they are not nearly as involved in politics as the self-identified Independents. In sum, one finds the following roughly linear progression of political involvement: (1) apoliticals; (2) no-preference neithers; (3) no-preference leaners; (4) pure Independents; and (5) Independent leaners. Therefore, the two no-preference groups should be considered separately as containing people who are detached from the party system but yet not uninterested enough in the political process as a whole to be classified as complete apoliticals. Because they differ from those who have traditionally been coded as apoliticals, as well as those who identify themselves as Independents, we will refer to them as "no-preference nonpartisans," so as

Table 3.2 Political involvement of nonpartisan groups, pooled 1964–1980 data (column percents)

	Apoliticals	No-preference neither	No-preference leaner	Independent neither	Independent leaner
Reported turnout					
Didn't vote	83.6	59.8	44.0	36.2	30.8
Voted	16.4	40.2	56.0	63.8	69.2
Frequency of voting					
Never	69.5	31.8	27.4	21.9	12.9
Sometimes	23.4	26.5	21.0	18.6	14.7
Most of the time	1.7	15.7	18.9	19.0	20.6
All of the time	5.4	26.0	32.6	40.6	51.8
Interest in the campaign					
Not much	80.8	43.4	29.5	31.5	19.9
Somewhat	17.3	41.9	44.3	43.2	45.6
Very much	1.9	14.7	26.3	25.3	34.6
Internal political efficacy					
Low (0–1)	79.6	70.4	66.6	63.1	50.8
High (2–3)	20.4	29.6	33.4	36.9	49.2

SOURCE: SRC/CPS National Election Studies.

to differentiate them from the categories obtained with the standard SRC/CPS coding scheme.

A Problem of Question Wording?

Perhaps, though, "no preference" is just what people say when they are confused by the choices in the standard party identification question. Following this line of reasoning, we might hypothesize that if no-preference nonpartisans were simply asked whether they ever considered themselves political Independents, they would acknowledge such an identity. Just such a question was in fact asked during the 1980 study in a section of the questionnaire separate from the usual party identification question. The results reveal some support for the above hypothesis, but the differences between the no-preference groups and the self-classified Independents are nevertheless quite marked. For example, only 24.5 percent of those who had "no preference" and leaned toward neither party responded that they sometimes considered themselves political Independents, compared to 75.4 percent of the respondents who called themselves "Independents" and leaned toward neither party. Similarly, only 38.4 percent of the no-preference leaners considered themselves to be political independents, compared to 82.7 percent of the Independent leaners.[10]

It is apparent, then, that the existence of this sizable block of no-preference nonpartisans is not simply an artifact of confused question wording. These respondents are distinct in their level of political involvement, and their attitudes toward political independence are different from those of self-professed Independents. Of course, it may be that these people could be readily categorized as a distinct group if the party identification question included a "no preference" option. Therefore, in this sense one can point to problems of question wording, in that the traditional version of the party identification scale does not provide an appropriate classification for these respondents.

Dissatisfaction with Parties or Indifference?

In order to develop a more complete understanding of party decline in the electorate, it is crucial to recognize that the proportion of people without a preference for the labels of Democrat, Republican, or Independent is both sizable and has been on the increase. Given that the growth in the proportion of no-preference nonpartisans has been so much more rapid than the growth of self-identified Independents, it is important to examine how differently the two groups perceive political parties. One possibility is that those with "no preference" are the most vehemently opposed to the political parties and dissatisfied with their performance. An alternative explanation is that these respondents do not perceive parties as relevant to the political process, and hence many of them do not consider themselves to be Independents simply because in their minds there are no meaningful partisan objects to be independent from.

Table 3.3 addresses both of these possibilities on the basis of three items that were asked about political parties in the 1980 CPS election study. One can test the first hypothesis by examining how the no-preference and Independent groups evaluate the job that the political parties are doing. Contrary to the hypothesis, the former group is actually more likely to feel that political parties are doing a good job for the country than the respondents who call

Table 3.3 Attitudes of nonpartisan groups toward political parties (column percents)

	No-preference neither	No-preference leaner	Independent neither	Independent leaner	Partisans
Job rating of political parties					
Good	31.1	26.5	9.2	18.5	24.4
Fair	31.1	40.8	46.0	35.6	41.4
Poor	37.8	32.7	44.8	45.8	34.2
The truth is, we probably don't need political parties in America anymore					
Disagree	35.7	36.5	44.5	47.3	63.5
Pro-con	18.6	14.3	10.0	12.4	10.2
Agree	45.7	49.2	45.5	40.3	26.2
It would be better if in all elections we put no party labels on the ballot					
Disagree	16.7	23.4	29.2	31.0	45.0
Pro-con	19.4	6.3	14.2	11.5	12.2
Agree	63.9	70.3	56.6	57.5	42.8

NOTE: Apoliticals are omitted here because of the small number of cases.
SOURCE: 1980 CPS National Election Study.

themselves Independents. Yet such a finding does not imply that the no-preference group sees parties as relevant in the governmental process; just the opposite seems to be the case. Elsewhere in the 1980 study people were asked whether they agreed or disagreed with the statement, "The truth is we probably don't need political parties in America anymore." On this question the no-preference individuals were actually somewhat less likely to recognize the importance of the parties in the political system by disagreeing with the statement. Similarly, these respondents were also less likely to disagree with the statement, "It would be better if in all elections we put no party labels on the ballot."[11]

They are therefore not so much dissatisfied with the parties as they are unaware of, or ambivalent about, the role they play in the political process. In contrast, respondents who classify themselves as Independents may be largely dissatisfied with the job that the parties are doing, and hence fail to identify with them, but many nevertheless feel that political parties perform a useful function.

The results of this chapter shed new light on the much-discussed decline of party identification in the United States. The proportion of the population labeling themselves as Independents has not risen nearly as much as has previously been thought, while the proportion with no preference has increased steadily over the last several elections. Such a finding has escaped notice in the literature to date because the traditional party identification scale does not provide any distinction between the two types of responses (unless someone with no preference is judged by the election study staff to be so little interested in politics as to warrant being classified as an apolitical).

Of course, if one defines political independence as simply not having a party affiliation, then the distinction is of little value. However, the concept of party identification is based on the premise that party represents a long-standing psychological predisposition that serves as an anchoring point for an individual's political attitudes. The statement that one considers oneself an Independent indicates that one is predisposed not to identify with or be bound to a political party. In contrast, a statement of "no preference" does not indicate any such predisposition.

It has been said that Americans are increasingly becoming turned off and tuned out with respect to political parties. However, the no-preference nonpartisans are evidently not turned off, although they are certainly tuned out. They are alienated in the sense that they lack integration into the party system and that they are less involved in politics than the self-classified Independents. Yet they show less dissatisfaction with the job that the parties are doing and score slightly higher on general measures of system support, such as trust in government, than do Independents. The growth in the proportion of the "no preference" response can be most plausibly interpreted as another indication of the declining salience of political parties in the American political process, which will be the focus of the next several chapters.

4
Negativity or Neutrality?

What has been found thus far about the decline of partisanship in the electorate suggests that political parties are substantially less important to the general public than they were two or three decades ago. Yet much of the literature on party decline in the electorate has postulated disenchantment with the parties as the major causal factor for the decline of partisanship. In *The Changing American Voter,* for example, Norman Nie, Sidney Verba, and John Petrocik argue that voters have come to view the parties in increasingly negative terms.[1]

The two explanations are not, of course, mutually exclusive. One reason the parties are less salient to people could be that they dislike both parties and therefore don't concern themselves much with either. However, it will be argued in this chapter that the increase in dissatisfaction with the parties has been minimal. The major change that has taken place in the public's evaluations of the parties has been that people feel neutral rather than negative. This is not to say that there has not been a decline of partisanship in the electorate, but instead that the nature of the decline has been different from what many have as-

sumed. The distinction is a crucial one for any understanding of the future of American political parties. If
voters are actually discontented with political parties,
then the parties' chances for recovery in the near future
are doubtful; but if people feel only neutral toward them,
then the door remains open for party renewal.

Indeed, a good deal of speculation on the future of the
political party system rests on the assumption that voters
have rejected parties. For example, Kristi Andersen writes
that a major difference between the 1920s and the 1970s is
that in the twenties those not affiliated with a party were
largely apathetic, while in the seventies "there appears to
be a more principled rejection of parties." Such a repu-
diation, she argues, will make the capture of Independents by one of the parties "exceedingly difficult."[2] It is
thus crucial to assess whether such a process has in fact
been responsible for party decline in the electorate.

An Examination of the Dissatisfaction Hypothesis

The dissatisfaction hypothesis about party decline in the
electorate contains two basic components. The first component is the assertion that voters increasingly see no important differences between the Democrats and the
Republicans. It has been said that the issues of the 1960s
cut across the traditional line of party cleavages and
blurred the distinction between the two major parties.[3] As
George Wallace said in 1968, "There's not a dime's worth
of difference between the two major parties." Second, it
has been presumed that because distrust of the government—that is, political cynicism—has risen concurrently
with independence, the two trends are related. One of the
clearest arguments for the joint impact of these causal

factors has been offered by Nie, Verba, and Petrocik. They attribute the increased expressions of disenchantment with the government to the troubles of the late 1960s and proceed to describe the following sequence of events: "The issues of the 1960s . . . do not clearly coincide with party lines; thus the parties offer no meaningful alternatives that might tie citizens more closely to them. Thus the political parties reap the results of the disaffection. Citizens come to look at the parties in more negative terms; they also begin to abandon the parties in greater numbers."[4]

The data available from the SRC/CPS election studies do not provide much support for such an interpretation, however. To begin with, as Table 4.1 shows, the proportion of respondents who thought that there were "important differences in what the Republican and Democratic parties stand for"[5] has remained quite stable over the years. Between 1952 and 1976 the proportion seeing important differences fluctuates minimally in the range from

Table 4.1 The electorate's perception of differences in what the two parties stand for

Year	Important differences	No differences, don't know[a]
1952	49.9	50.1
1960	50.3	49.7
1964	50.8	49.2
1968	52.0	48.0
1972	46.1	53.9
1976	47.2	52.8
1980	58.0	42.0

a. In 1964 and 1968 "don't know" was not on the questionnaire; thus the percentage coded as "no difference" was artificially inflated. To make all results comparable, I have combined responses of "no difference" and "don't know."

46 to 52 percent. The data for 1980 show a significant change from 1976, but it is in the opposite direction from what would be predicted by the dissatisfaction hypothesis: in 1980, 58 percent perceived important differences between the parties. It is interesting to note that public perception of party differences was more widespread in 1980 than in either 1964 or 1972, years when, as most scholars would undoubtedly agree, the differences were in reality even sharper.

Nevertheless, the fact that the electorate continues to see important differences in what the parties stand for does not necessarily mean that citizens continue to see the differences as meaning anything in terms of government performance. Since 1960 the election studies have asked respondents what they consider to be the most important problem facing the country. Those who mention a problem are subsequently asked which of the two parties would be the most likely to do what they want on this problem.[6] As can be seen in Table 4.2, the percentage who

Table 4.2 Percent seeing one of the parties as doing the best job on the problem they considered most important

Year	Party mentioned[a]	About the same	Don't know
1960	62.0	25.0	13.0
1964	65.7	25.3	9.0
1968	51.6	38.7[b]	9.8
1972	49.0	42.4	8.6
1976	46.3	46.0	7.7
1980	50.3	42.7	7.1

a. These respondents mentioned either the Democratic or the Republican party.

b. Included are those who saw no difference between the major parties but believed that Wallace would do what they wanted.

SOURCE: SRC/CPS National Election Studies.

feel that one of the parties will do better on the problem that most concerns them has declined since 1964. In that year 65.7 percent thought that one party would be the more likely to do what they wanted, even though only 50.8 percent said that there were important differences in what the parties stood for. In contrast, in 1980 only 50.3 percent thought that one party would be better on the problem they considered most important—which for the first time was significantly lower than the proportion seeing important differences between the parties.

One possible interpretation of this finding is that it represents a growing disenchantment with political parties and the government in general. Merle Black and George Rabinowitz, for instance, note that this pattern bears a striking similarity to trends in trust in government. They write, "If neither party can provide desirable alternative solutions to the problems an individual feels are most important for the government to do something about, it is reasonable for the individual to view the parties unfavorably and lose faith in the government."[7] According to such an interpretation, respondents may still see major differences between the parties but many are so dissatisfied with the opposing alternatives that they have become alienated.

However, those respondents who believe that there wouldn't be any difference between the parties in handling the problem they feel is most important are no more cynical than those who believe that there would be a difference. On a cynicism scale ranging from +100 to −100, the former group is never more than two points more cynical than the latter. In fact, those respondents who feel that there would be no difference between the parties are actually somewhat less cynical in both 1976 and 1980 than their counterparts in these years.

Such a null finding brings into question whether there is any relationship between the respective declines in partisanship and trust in government, as is often presumed. One simple way to establish whether there is such a relationship is to correlate the cynicism scale with strength of party identification. Only in 1968 is there a relationship worth noting. The Pearson correlation between the two variables varies from a high of .11 in 1968 to a low of −.02 in 1972, averaging about .04. It is plausible to infer, therefore, that the initial declines in both party identification and trust in government between 1965 and 1968 were *slightly* intertwined, but there has been no consistent relationship between the two variables.

Yet cross-sectional data can hide systematic changes over time. As Nie et al. emphasize, panel data are necessary for establishing or rejecting a causal link. Fortunately, one panel is now available in which there are substantial declines in both party identification and trust in government—the 1965–1973 Jennings-Niemi socialization panel.[8] This dataset is particularly interesting because it contains a large sample of new entrants into the electorate who have contributed so much to the growth of the nonpartisan group.[9]

If it is true that the decline in party identification is due to the growth of cynicism toward the government, then it would be expected that those in the panel who became more distrusting between 1965 and 1973 would also be the respondents who showed the greatest decline in partisanship. As Table 4.3 demonstrates, however, this was not the case. For example, data on the younger generation (first interviewed as high school seniors in 1965) show that there was a substantial decline in strength of party identification in every cell of the table with very little variation depending on whether the cell represents those

Table 4.3 Change in strength of party identification by change in cynicism toward the government

YOUTH

1965 cynicism	1973 cynicism		
	Trusting	In between	Cynical
Trusting	−24.4[a]	−36.3	−18.5
(N)	(206)	(307)	(281)
In between	−16.3	−29.4	−22.1
(N)	(49)	(108)	(160)
Cynical	—[b]	−24.8	−30.2
(N)	(8)	(28)	(63)

PARENTS

1965 cynicism	1973 cynicism		
	Trusting	In between	Cynical
Trusting	− 9.9	+ 4.3	−13.9
(N)	(153)	(206)	(137)
In between	+ 2.1	−12.2	0.0
(N)	(51)	(132)	(157)
Cynical	—[b]	− 6.1	−17.7
(N)	(16)	(84)	(154)

a. Table entries represent change in strength of party identification from 1965 to 1973. Strength of party identification is calculated by scoring the percentage of Strong Democrats and Strong Republicans as +2, Weak Democrats and Weak Republicans as +1, Independent Democrats and Republicans as 0, and Pure Independents and Apoliticals as −1.

b. Insufficient data.

SOURCE: Jennings-Niemi Socialization Panel Study.

whose cynicism score increased, stayed the same, or decreased. Even the youth who were *least* cynical in both years showed a sizable decline of 24.4 points on strength of partisanship. In comparison, those who shifted from trusting to cynical during the eight-year interval showed only an 18.5 point drop. For the parents the decline in strength of party identification was much smaller, but there is a similar lack of any consistent pattern of changes by cynicism scores. Indeed, some of the cells show changes that are the reverse of what would be expected. The absence of any systematic pattern of changes in the data is best demonstrated by the near-zero correlation between each individual's score on a change in strength of party identification measure (ranging from +3 to −3) and a change in cynicism score (ranging from +5 to −5). These correlations are .01 for the youth cohort and −.01 for the parents.

Thus there is no evidence in this panel to suggest that the rise in cynicism has been responsible for the decline of party identification. It must be concluded that the growth of cynicism and nonpartisanship are roughly parallel trends that have little relationship to each other in both a static and a dynamic sense.

What has been found thus far in this chapter suggests that a reexamination of citizens' attitudes toward the parties is in order. The dissatisfaction hypothesis depends largely on two assumptions—that voters no longer see important differences in what the parties stand for, and that the decline in strength of party identification has been an outgrowth of the decay of public trust in the government—for which little support has been found here.

It is true that there has been a decline in the percentage of the electorate which believes that one party would do a better job in handling whatever they perceive to be the most important governmental problem. However, the fact that such feelings are not related to political distrust indicates that this trend may not necessarily be a reflection of negative attitudes toward the parties. An equally plausible alternative explanation is that citizens simply see the parties as less relevant than in the past, and hence citizens' feelings toward them are more neutral than negative. With the growth of the mass media and candidate-centered campaigns, the importance of parties in the presidential selection process and in government in general has been weakened. The ideological differences between the parties may remain, but on the crucial short-run policy issues of the day it is the candidates that now matter most. Because of these changes there is reason to expect that the electorate should be less positive about the two parties than in the past but that the shift in attitudes will be toward neutrality rather than negativity. Just such a possibility will be examined next.

An Evaluative Perspective on Party Decline

One major weakness in the literature on party decline is that the research has been nearly wholly concerned with the affective (party identification) and behavioral (voting by party line) aspects of the electorate's relationship to political parties. This is not to demean the importance of the decline in strength of party identification and straight-ticket voting; clearly these trends may have significant systemic consequences, most notably the rise in political volatility and instability in the United States. The problem is that such trends have been grafted onto the description of the evaluative dimension of parties as well without proper evidence. That more people choose not to call themselves Democrats or Republicans may not necessarily mean that they are "rejecting" parties, or, as James Sundquist puts it, "calling down a plague on both their houses."[10] Similarly, choosing to split one's ticket also may not imply a long-term rejection of the parties, but rather may simply mean that people no longer view the candidates in partisan terms.

What is sorely lacking is an analysis of just how positive, neutral, or negative Americans are toward the parties and what they like or dislike about them. It is such an evaluative approach that will be presented here. In every presidential election year since 1952 the SRC/CPS election studies have asked respondents in the preelection wave what they liked and disliked about the two political parties. Up to five responses have been coded in each year for each of the four questions.[11] By simply subtracting the number of negative comments from the number of positive ones, respondents can then be classified as either positive, neutral, or negative toward each of the parties, depending on whether the number of likes is greater than, equal to, or less than the number of dislikes.

After collapsing the data into negative, neutral, and positive ratings on each of the two parties, a sixfold classification representing respondents' ratings of both parties was created. The six categories are as follows: (1) *negative-negative,* those who have negative attitudes toward both parties; (2) *negative-neutral,* those who report negative ratings of one party, a neutral evaluation of the other; (3) *neutral-neutral,* those who are neutral with respect to both parties; (4) *positive-negative,* those who report a positive evaluation of one party, a negative evaluation of the other; (5) *positive-neutral,* those who are positive toward one party and neutral toward the other; and (6) *positive-positive,* those who rate both parties in a positive fashion. It should be noted that in all of these categories which party the respondent feels warm, neutral, or cold toward is irrelevant. For example, some of the positive-negative respondents rate the Democrats positively and the Republicans negatively and some vice versa, but what is important here is that these respondents see the parties in a polarized warm-cool fashion, not which party they feel positive toward.

The percentages of respondents falling into the six categories on the basis of these like/dislike questions from 1952 to 1980 are shown in Table 4.4. If it is true that citizens are disenchanted with the parties and have come to perceive them in far more negative terms than in the past, then we would expect to find a large increase in the proportion of negative-negatives and negative-neutrals in the post-1964 period. Certainly this is the case in 1968, the first measurement point available after party identification began to decline. From 1964 to 1968 there is a 5.6 percent increase in those negative toward both parties and a 2.6 percent rise in the negative-neutral category. Given that party identification continued to erode after 1968, it might be hypothesized that the percentage of the electorate with negative attitudes toward the parties would also continue to rise. However, the data clearly shows just the reverse. Between 1968 and 1980 both the negative-negatives and negative-neutrals declined. Thus, the 1968 election stands out as an aberrant year with respect to negative attitudes about the parties, rather than the beginning of a trend.

What does change dramatically after 1968 involves the large increase of the neutral-neutrals and the decline of polarized partisans, that is, the positive-negatives. In 1968 the proportion of polarized partisans was over twice that of the neutral-neutrals; in both 1972 and 1976 the proportion of neutral-neutrals is roughly equal, and in 1980 over 9 percent higher. But what is most fascinating about Table 4.4 is that the increase of those having neutral attitudes to-

Table 4.4 Trends in the public's evaluations of the two major parties

Year	Negative-negative	Negative-neutral	Neutral-neutral	Positive-negative	Positive-neutral	Positive-positive
1952	3.6	9.7	13.0	50.1	18.1	5.5
1956	2.9	9.0	15.9	40.0	23.3	8.9
1960	1.9	7.5	16.8	41.4	24.2	8.3
1964	4.4	11.2	20.2	38.4	20.6	5.0
1968	10.0	13.8	17.3	37.5	17.4	4.1
1972	7.9	12.6	29.9	30.3	14.7	4.7
1976	7.5	11.8	31.3	31.1	13.7	4.5
1980	5.0	8.6	36.5	27.3	17.7	4.8

SOURCE: SRC/CPS National Election Studies.

ward both parties is a trend that is evident throughout the entire twenty-eight-year period—in the "steady state" period as well as in the period of weakening ties to the parties. From 1952 to 1964, while strength of party identification showed little change, the proportion of neutral-neutrals increased with each election, from 13.0 percent in 1952 to 20.2 percent in 1964. Only in 1968 is the linearity of the trend broken because of the largely short-term increase in negativity toward the parties in that year.

It is also evident from the table that the decline of polarized partisans began well before strength of party identification started to drop off. This is especially apparent between 1952 and 1956, when the proportion of positive-negatives fell by over 10 percent. One would intuitively have to hypothesize that the issues of the New Deal, which the party system is generally considered to have been aligned upon, were sharply declining in salience from 1952 to 1956. Through 1960 many of these positive-negatives apparently moved to the less polarized categories of positive-neutral and positive-positive, both of which reached their high points during the years of the Eisenhower presidency. But after 1960 these groups declined in numbers, as did the positive-negatives. Overall, from 1952 to 1980 the percentage of positive-negatives fell from 50.1 to 27.3 percent. Except for the slight increase during the Eisenhower years, the percentage of those positive toward both parties remained fairly stable at about 5 percent.

Given the evidence from Table 4.4, the reader may wonder how Nie, Verba, and Petrocik concluded that citizens had come to look upon parties in more negative terms—especially because they also analyzed responses to the party like/dislike questions.[12] The answer simply is that

Nie et al. combined the categories of negative-negative, negative-neutral, and neutral-neutral into a single group that they labeled variously as "negative evaluations of both parties," "alienated from the parties," or "nonsupporters of the parties." Only the third phrase is an accurate description of what they were measuring. To infer that a neutral evaluation of the parties represents dissatisfaction is to make an extremely tenuous assumption, especially since the growth of neutrality on these open-ended questions has been entirely due to the increase (from 9.7 to 34.3 percent) in the proportion of the population who have nothing at all to say—either positive or negative—about either party, and hence end up being classified as neutral toward both.[13]

Additional Evidence from Feeling Thermometers

Another point that Nie et al. make about the increase in negative attitudes concerns the decline over time in the public's feeling thermometer ratings of the parties. As shown in Figure 4.1, the mean rating of "Democrats" has fallen by about eight points since 1964, and the mean rating of "Republicans" shortly after the Reagan victory in 1980 was actually lower than during the Goldwater debacle in 1964.

But do lower ratings necessarily indicate the presence of more intense negative evaluations? Because feeling thermometer ratings represent a summary of both positive and negative affect, the trends shown in Figure 4.1 could just as easily be due to a decline in positive feelings as to a rise in negative ones. Furthermore, it is quite possible that if *both* positive and negative feelings were to decline in intensity, the net result would be a lower mean

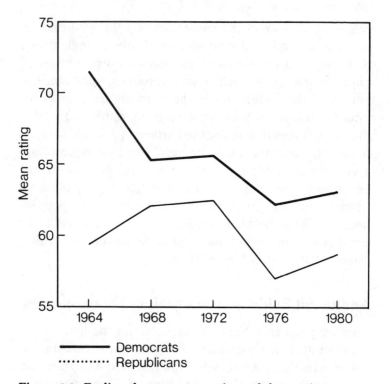

Figure 4.1 Feeling thermometer ratings of the parties, 1964–1980
Source: SRC/CPS National Election Studies.

rating. This is because of the positivity bias that is usually associated with the feeling thermometer instrument. For example, on the like/dislike measure one never finds more than 9 percent of the population giving a positive evaluation of both parties (see Table 4.4), while an average of nearly 40 percent rate both parties at above the neutral point—that is, 50 degrees—on the feeling thermometer. Thus one could find people who are positive as well as those who are negative gravitating equally toward the neutral point, but the fact that the distributions are so heavily skewed toward the positive side means that there will be more downward than upward movement.

From Table 4.5 we can see that such a decline in the intensity of *both* positive and negative feelings toward the parties has in fact taken place. Those who give favorable ratings now give less favorable ones than in the past. Similarly, respondents who give negative ratings are now less intensely negative than in the mid-1960s. These trends are best summarized by taking the absolute value of the distance of the ratings from 50 degrees. In 1964 the average respondent evaluated the two parties such that the combined distance of both ratings from the neutral point was 46.1 points (26.5 for ratings of "Democrats" plus 19.6 for ratings of "Republicans").[14] By 1976 the comparable figure

Table 4.5 Trends in the intensity of feeling thermometer ratings of the parties

	1964	1968	1972	1976	1980
Rating of "Democrats"					
Average distance above 50 degrees for those positive	34.0	29.9	26.2	24.4	25.5
Average distance below 50 degrees for those negative	24.0	22.5	17.1	17.0	18.1
Average distance from 50 degrees (includes those at 50)	26.5	21.3	19.1	15.5	17.5
Rating of "Republicans"					
Average distance above 50 degrees for those positive	28.4	27.2	25.1	21.6	21.8
Average distance below 50 degrees for those negative	26.5	25.1	22.7	19.7	20.6
Average distance from 50 degrees (includes those at 50)	19.6	18.9	18.2	12.7	14.6

SOURCE: SRC/CPS National Election Studies.

had fallen by nearly 40 percent to 28.2. There is a slight increase between 1976 and 1980 in the intensity of feeling thermometer ratings of the parties, but it hardly represents a major reversal of the trend.[15] The overall picture is clearly one of movement toward the neutral point from both the positive and negative sides of the scale.

In sum, the results from both the like/dislike responses and the feeling thermometers reinforce one another despite their methodological differences. In each the major trend is a growing neutrality in the electorate's perception of the parties. The fact that similar trends can be found with disparate sets of data provides a pleasing confirmation of the theoretical framework outlined above.

A Comparison of Party Images in 1952 and 1980

Just how fragile the current party alignment has become because of the rise in neutrality can be illustrated by the lack of substance in respondents' party images, as revealed in the 1980 election study. As Table 4.6 demonstrates, the only major advantage enjoyed by either party is the positive image of the groups that the Democrats are perceived as representing. Similarly, the only major disadvantage for either party is the negative image that people have of the groups popularly associated with the Republican Party. These feelings that the Democrats are the party of the common working man while the Republicans are the party of the upper class and big business represent virtually the last remnant of the images of the parties that developed during the New Deal era.

Table 4.7 presents an examination of the party images found in the 1952 election study, which can be directly compared to the percentages displayed in Table 4.6 for

Table 4.6 Images of the political parties, 1980

Because of:	Like Democrats	Dislike Democrats	Like Republicans	Dislike Republicans
The groups they are for or against	25.5	4.2	4.3	19.3
Economic/welfare policy stands	6.2	10.0	8.1	3.9
Social issue stands	0.8	0.7	1.0	1.1
Stands on general philosophy of government activity	8.1	8.2	11.1	5.1
Their ability to manage the government	2.5	9.7	7.2	2.0
Foreign policy	4.2	6.3	7.4	4.5
Carter	0.6	1.9	—	—
Reagan	—	—	1.1	1.5

NOTE: Table entries are the proportion of the sample offering each given type of response.
SOURCE: 1980 CPS National Election Study.

Table 4.7 Images of the political parties, 1952

Because of:	Like Democrats	Dislike Democrats	Like Republicans	Dislike Republicans
The groups they are for or against	33.1	4.7	3.2	20.3
Economic/welfare policy stands	31.9	16.3	22.1	22.4
Social issue stands	—	—	—	—
Stands on general philosophy of government activity	11.4	8.7	11.0	5.8
Their ability to manage the government	2.3	26.6	18.0	4.3
Foreign policy	4.1	17.1	12.3	3.4
Truman	1.0	7.6	—	—
Eisenhower	—	—	7.7	1.8
Stevenson	1.3	0.9	—	—

SOURCE: 1952 SRC National Election Study.

1980. The comparison indicates that there has been a marked deterioration of images that once were highly favorable to the Democrats and of those that once greatly benefited the Republicans. Leaving aside the long-standing impressions of which parties favor which groups, the electorate just no longer has much to say when asked what they like and dislike about the two parties.

In 1952, for example, nearly a third of the respondents stated that they liked the Democratic Party because of its economic or welfare policies, while 22 percent made negative comments along those lines in reference to the Republicans. With memories of the Depression now in the distant past, it is probably not too surprising to find that the comparable figures in 1980 were only 6 and 4 percent, respectively. Many observers may be surprised to find, however, that positive comments about the Republican Party's economic/welfare policy stands were also more numerous in the 1952 sample than in 1980 (22 percent compared to 8 percent). Moreover, despite the poor performance of the economy during the Carter administration, only 10 percent of those interviewed made negative comments about the economic and welfare policies of the Democratic Party. In sum, neither party now has a very firmly entrenched positive or negative public image on such issues compared to two or three decades ago.[16]

In the areas of foreign policy and management of the government, the images of the parties are also not nearly as clearly defined as they once were. In both 1952 and 1980 the Republicans were perceived favorably on these dimensions while the Democrats were viewed negatively because of dissatisfaction with the performances of Truman and Carter, respectively. The key difference to note is that in 1980 such feelings were far less salient than in

1952. The fact that only 7 percent of those interviewed made positive comments about the Republicans on each of these dimensions in 1980 hardly constitutes a resounding statement of faith in Republican foreign policies or management capabilities. Nor is there any indication that Carter's failures in these areas are likely to have a long-term negative impact on the Democratic Party, as the comparable negative figures in 1952 were nearly three times as high.

That the Democratic Party largely escaped blame for the entire range of problems of the Carter administration, from the economy to Iran, might be interpreted as an incredible stroke of good fortune, especially considering that such problems were quite prevalent in open-ended evaluations of Jimmy Carter in 1980. However, such a pattern is more likely a symptom of the dissociation of public perceptions of candidates and presidents from the political parties that they nominally represent. With the rise of the plebiscitary presidency and the growth of the mass media, candidates no longer need the parties to convey their messages and voters are now able to see for themselves just what the candidates are like. A number of recent presidential campaigns—most notably that of Richard Nixon in 1972—have thus been able to consciously downplay partisan appeals.

In 1980 neither candidate really made any effort to avoid party associations, however. Reagan clearly attempted to be more of a Republican team man than any nominee in the party's recent history, and Carter stressed his Democratic affiliation to the utmost given that his low approval ratings made it difficult to offer much else in the way of a positive appeal. In spite of these strategies, very few people evaluated the parties in 1980 on the basis of their standard-bearers, as shown in Table 4.6. For example, only 1 percent of the sample stated that they liked the Republicans because of Ronald Reagan. Whether this figure will be much greater in the future if the Reagan program succeeds remains to be seen, but if so it would mark a reversal of the historical trend that will be the major focus of the following chapter. In this candidate-centered media age, people have apparently become less accustomed to praising or blaming the parties for presidential performance.

The results presented in this chapter offer somewhat more hope for the revitalization of American political parties than most previous work on the subject. However, one can also extrapolate reasons to be doubtful about such a prospect, based on the interpretation of party decline that has been argued here.

Taking the positive side first, the most important new piece of data is that there has been little increase in the proportion of the population holding negative attitudes toward the parties. It is conceivable that the initial decline in strength of party identification may have been due to the large jump in negativity apparent in 1968. But since that time negative attitudes toward the parties have subsided. Positive attitudes have also continued to decline, but what has increased has been neutrality rather than negativity.

Besides the fact that parties do not have to overcome largely negative attitudes toward them, it is also encouraging to note that their recovery probably does not hinge on a restoration of trust in government. Like other institutions, political parties are viewed more cynically than in the past. However, this sort of cynicism is apparently not being translated into negative attitudes. People may be more skeptical about the motives of parties, but that does not necessarily mean that they dislike parties in general or that they will not identify with a party in the future. This point is supported by the fact that hardly any relationship was found between strength of party identification and trust in government, except for the .11 correlation in 1968. And in a dynamic sense, panel data show that the two trends are quite independent of one another. Given that the decline of partisanship has been a reflection of growing neutrality instead of negativity, such null findings are quite explicable. If negative attitudes about parties were at the root of the rise of nonpartisanship then one would expect that other negative attitudes such as cynicism would be related to it, as indeed the case of 1968 appears to show. But overall the evidence demonstrates that the decline of parties in the electorate has been more a function of a reduction in saliency than an increase in negative attitudes.

However, turning to the reasons to be pessimistic about any revitalization of parties in the electorate, there seems to be little prospect for reversing the trend toward neutrality in the immediate future. One of the most important findings in this chapter is that the decline of parties in the electorate can be traced back much further than the mid-1960s in terms of party evaluations. The decline of polarized views of the parties and the increase in neutrality is visible throughout the election study time series. Thus it can undoubtedly be considered a long-term secular trend, and such trends are usually difficult to reverse.

5
Political Leadership and the Parties

The analytical problem, as defined by the growth in neutrality described in the preceding chapter, is to explain why political parties are now less important to the public than in the past. It will be helpful, therefore, to consider what elements of the political world influence the salience of concepts such as partisanship in the first place. A useful starting point can be found in the chapter on membership in social groupings in *The American Voter*. Campbell, Converse, Miller, and Stokes write:

> Political salience . . . refers to any heightening of awareness of a particular group membership at the time when the individual is oriented to the political world. This dimension . . . is especially subject to short-term variation, since salience usually depends on the most transient objects of political orientation: the candidates and the issues.
>
> Political salience of the group is high, for example, when a candidate for the election is recognized as a member of the group.[1]

In other words, without candidates and issues with which political parties can be identified, the salience of partisanship in the electorate is likely to suffer. The key variable is of course leadership, for the link between issues and parties depends heavily on the candidate's actions, that is, his or her treatment of issues in partisan terms—stressing that as a Democrat or a Republican he or she stands for certain ideas and policies. It is thus crucial to note that for a variety of institutional reasons candidates now have substantially less incentive to foster the link between themselves and the parties, as well as between political issues and the parties. As Lester Seligman has written, "Deprived of presidential support, political parties are losing their meaning to the voters. Increasingly, Presidents are no longer making political parties and parties are no longer making Presidents."[2]

At the outset of this book it was noted that recruiting and nominating candidates is one of the functions that political parties are called on to perform. In fact, back in the days when parties still played a central role in selecting presidential candidates, E. E. Schattschneider singled out this function as perhaps the most crucial of all. "Unless the party makes authoritative and effective nominations, it cannot stay in business," wrote Schattschneider. "The nature of the nominating procedure determines the nature of the party."[3] More recently, former Congressman Donald Fraser has taken a similar point of view. He writes, "To the extent that the organized party abdicates responsibility for the selection of its candidates, it becomes almost irrelevant to the solution of the problems facing our nation."[4]

The deterioration of the traditional role of parties in the presidential selection process has been thoroughly documented in the literature and need not be reviewed in detail for our purposes.[5] Basically, the crux of the change has been to alter the constituency on which candidates are dependent for nomination from the party organization regulars to the public at large and the mass media.

At first, the strategy of conducting a candidate-centered media campaign to develop a candidate's popular appeal was effective largely to the extent to which it fostered support among the party leaders. For example, John F. Kennedy's victories in several key Democratic primaries in 1960 were an important factor in his nomination, but without the support he gathered from the party leaders he would in all likelihood have met the same fate as Estes Kefauver—who won twelve of thirteen primaries in 1952 yet lost the nomination fight as a direct result of opposition from the party leadership.[6]

Since 1968, however, the proportion of convention delegates selected via primary elections has risen from about one-third to four-fifths, thereby making the accumulation of primary votes the key to nomination. In addition, the delegates selected in caucuses are no longer as organizationally oriented as in the past, for the caucus process has been substantially opened in order to forestall leadership manipulation. Comparing primary and caucus-selected delegates, Barbara Farah finds virtually no differences between the two in terms of orientation to party or representativeness.[7] Indeed, it is the open caucus in Iowa, as much as the New Hampshire and other early primaries, which now performs the function of narrowing down the presidential field. Those candidates who fare poorly in Iowa, New Hampshire, and the other early contests receive only minimal attention in the media and are soon written off as serious contenders.[8] Where once the organizational leaders played the role of talent scouts and assessors based on past performance in governing, reporters now do so based on performance in caucuses and primaries.

The net result of the many changes in the nomination process has led Austin Ranney to dub the new process aptly as "closely approaching a no-party system." His summary of the current state of affairs is instructive and worth quoting at length:

Presidential nominations are contested by candidate-centered organizations. Each organization is assembled by the candidate and his inner circle. Each is financed in part by funds it raises and in part by federal matching funds . . . Each appeals to the party rank and file in primaries, caucuses, and conventions with little concern for what the state organizational leaders do or don't do. The party organizations simply are not actors in presidential politics. Indeed, they are little more than custodians of the party-label prize which goes to the winning candidate organization. The parties have long since ceased to be judges *awarding* the prize.[9]

Not only do parties—as institutions—now play a greatly reduced role in nominating and electing the president, they also have been pushed out of the public spotlight in terms of actual governing. Presidents have always had a tendency to try to bypass parties once in office by appealing to the national interest and to the people as a whole, but the growth of the Executive branch has made such a strategy eminently more feasible and rewarding. Since the start of the New Deal the number of White House aides has grown from about the size of the Supreme Court to that of the U.S. Congress. More than one hundred of these aides are now involved in some form of public relations, according to Cronin—"busily selling and reselling the President."[10] Furthermore, there are presidential assistants to deal with virtually every major policy area and to build lines of support with virtually all existing interest groups. As Hugh Heclo has written, "If one were inventing a political party, these are exactly the types of offices at branch headquarters that one would want to create. What is lacking is only the local cells that would give such an organization feet and hands."[11]

Turning to the congressional level, changes have also occurred so as to make the public less likely to link parties with candidates and issues. Here, there is empirical evidence indicating that members of Congress are increasingly acting in a less partisan manner. As Figure 5.1 shows, the percentage of party-line votes cast in the House of Representatives has steadily fallen from one administration to the next. During the years when Franklin Roosevelt was in office the majority of Democrats voted in opposition to the majority of Republicans on nearly 60 percent of all the recorded roll calls; by the Nixon-Ford years this figure had dropped to under 35 percent. A small increase in party-line voting did occur in Carter's term, but in part this may just be a reflection of the fact that the Democrats once again controlled both the presidency and Congress, as divided control tends to foster somewhat less partisan behavior.

Of course, it would be out of the question to assume that the mass public is really very aware of this decline in party voting in Congress. However, the public is exposed to the new style of congressional campaigning—a style that fits in nicely with this quantitative evidence of increasingly less partisan behavior once elected to office. As Fiorina has argued, the growth of the Washington bureaucratic establishment has enabled members of Congress to

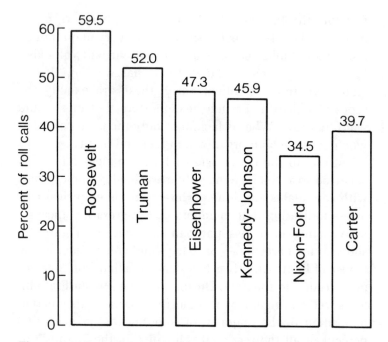

Figure 5.1   Party-line voting in the House from Roosevelt to Carter

Note: Percentages shown represent averages for the Congresses during each administration or combination of administrations.

Sources: Data for 1932–1976 taken from David W. Brady and Charles S. Bullock III, "Coalition Politics in the House of Representatives," in Lawrence C. Dodd and Bruce I. Oppenheimer, eds., *Congress Reconsidered,* 2d ed. (Washington, D.C.: Congressional Quarterly Press, 1981). Percentage for the Carter administration calculated by the author from Congressional Quarterly Reports for these years.

run for office as ombudsmen, assisting constituents with problems with the federal government and bringing home pork-barrel projects for the district.[12] Such activities are noncontroversial, and hence can only aid one's reelection. More important, they are also nonpartisan. The result, no doubt, is that many voters have come to feel that if their representative is doing a good job helping out people in the district then it shouldn't matter whether he or she is a Democrat or a Republican.

Public Evaluations of Parties and Candidates

To investigate whether these changes have in fact been reflected by a change in the public's evaluations of the relationship between parties and candidates, we need to examine comparable time series data concerning each from the election studies. Such data are available in the form of the traditional open-ended questions, which ask respondents what they like and dislike about the two parties and whether there is anything in particular that might make them vote for or against the two major presidential candidates. As utilized elsewhere in this work, counting the number of positive responses and then subtracting the number of negative ones yields a summary score of net affect toward each party and candidate. And as Figure 5.2 demonstrates, the correlation between party and candidate evaluations has indeed declined over the years. The correlation between ratings of Carter and the Democratic Party in 1980 represents the weakest relationship between public perceptions of a candidate and his party in the historical time series, and on the Republican side only ratings of Gerald Ford were less related to Republican Party evaluations than those of Ronald Reagan. Most revealing of all, however, is the secular decline in the correlation between the partisan direction (that is, affect toward Democrats minus affect toward Republicans) of candidate and party evaluations from .70 in 1952 to .54 in 1980—or, in terms of common variance, from 49 to 29 percent.

In part, this change is probably attributable to the fact

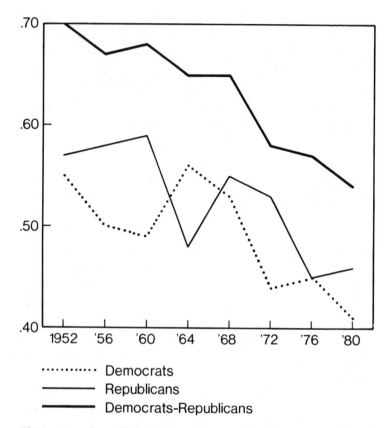

.... Democrats
——— Republicans
——— Democrats-Republicans

Figure 5.2 Correlations between party and candidate like/dislike measures, 1952–1980
Source: SRC/CPS National Election Studies.

that spontaneous references to party affiliation in response to the candidate questions have declined substantially over the years.[13] For example, 15.7 percent of those interviewed in 1952 said that they either liked or disliked Stevenson because he was a Democrat and 9.5 percent expressed a like or dislike of Eisenhower because he was a Republican. By comparison, only 2.9 percent mentioned Carter's party affiliation in 1980 and 4.1 percent mentioned Reagan's.

But *why* are parties and candidates less tightly linked in public perceptions than in the past? Theoretically, what should bind the two together is a commonality in issue stands. Knowing a candidate's party affiliation alone should give the citizen an issue basis for evaluation of the candidate. Under such a framework issues are largely partisan matters which get translated at election time into assessments of candidates, rather than being transient concerns which are primarily candidate-centered. Given the historical changes discussed above, however, there is good reason to believe that the latter pattern may well have become more prevalent than the former.

It will be recalled from Chapter 4 that when respondents are asked which major party would do best in solving whatever they consider to be the most important problem of the day, an increasing proportion have been responding that there would be no difference. This trend cannot be explained by an increase in the perception that there are no longer important differences between the parties, for there has not been any such increase. Nor can it be attributed to the decline in trust in government. Thus it might be hypothesized that more citizens are now conceptualizing issues in terms of candidates only and less in terms of party alone. In other words, the stands that candidates take on the issues may no longer be linked to voters' perceptions of the parties. The parties may still stand for certain broad principles and groups, but when it comes to specific policies, candidates now stand *above* parties rather than with them.

To test this hypothesis, we can compare the frequency

of responses to the candidate like/dislike questions to the frequency of likes and dislikes expressed about the parties on four substantive dimensions or response categories: domestic issues, foreign issues, benefits provided to groups, and general political philosophy.[14] If such a hypothesis is correct, then one would expect an increase over time in the proportion of the population commenting about issues with respect to the candidates but not with respect to parties. Such a pattern would indicate that issues are irrelevant to the citizen in evaluating parties but relevant with regard to the candidates.

Table 5.1 provides evidence that such a pattern has become much more prevalent over the years, especially on domestic and foreign policy. For example, domestic issues were overwhelmingly associated with the parties in 1952, with only 2.7 percent making such comments with reference only to candidates, compared to 53.5 percent for parties only. But by 1964 the balance had shifted dramatically to the point where more respondents were mentioning domestic issues only in terms of candidates than parties only, and in 1980 the ratio is over two to one in favor of the candidate-only response pattern. References to parties and candidates on foreign policy were roughly balanced in 1952, but the same trend is nevertheless apparent. By 1964 the percentage in the candidate-only category was twice that of the party-only group, and in 1980 41.6 percent of the sample mentioned foreign policy in reference to a candidate but not with respect to either party, while only 3.5 percent displayed the reverse pattern. Finally, while there is a slight decrease in the party-only response pattern for the dimensions of group benefits and general philosophy of government, these attitudes still remain predominantly the domain of the parties, and thus probably account for the lack of any drop in the percentage of the population perceiving major differences between the parties.

One particularly interesting feature of these data is that because they are based on preelection information, they refer in large part to the politics of the previous four years and are usually influenced only in minor part by nonincumbent candidacies. Thus the 1952 data can be seen as capturing the perceived importance of parties over candidates that had developed by the last of the New Deal administrations, and the change that occurred between 1952 and 1956 suggests the extent to which the Eisenhower presidency diminished the salience of party on domestic and foreign issues. Eisenhower's distrust of partisanship and his "above party" stance were well known and undoubtedly had a major effect on the public's conceptualization of the issues. As he himself stated during a 1954 press conference: "I think it is quite apparent that I am not very much of a partisan. The times are too serious, I think, to indulge in partisanship to the extreme."[15] The virtual identicalness of the 1956 and 1960 figures reflect quite properly that the perceptions put into place by the first four years of the Eisenhower presidency simply persisted over the next four. Between 1960 and 1964, however, the most dramatic four-year change can be seen on domestic issues, in part due to Goldwater's extraordinarily issue-oriented campaign but also indicating that after four years of the Kennedy-Johnson administrations the linking of domestic issues with party had been dealt another severe blow. Strong leadership overshadowed the parties and hence issues became further personified. Goldwater's disappearance from the national scene and the partisan controversy stirred by the implementation of

Table 5.1 The frequency of substantive responses to the party and candidate like/dislike questions

	Mentioned for neither	Mentioned for party only	Mentioned for candidate only	Mentioned for both
Domestic issues				
1952	36.7	53.5	2.7	7.1
1956	49.9	31.8	7.8	10.4
1960	51.7	31.0	7.2	10.1
1964	46.8	15.9	20.5	16.7
1968	54.1	22.0	11.2	12.7
1972	49.6	14.2	21.6	14.7
1976	50.9	19.8	16.6	12.7
1980	46.6	11.0	27.7	14.7
Foreign issues				
1952	55.6	17.4	16.2	10.8
1956	59.9	12.1	16.8	11.2
1960	56.9	13.1	18.8	11.1
1964	64.3	9.0	19.5	7.2
1968	54.7	13.9	20.0	11.4
1972	46.1	6.6	39.1	8.2
1976	74.3	9.1	11.5	5.1
1980	46.0	3.5	41.6	8.8

Benefits provided to groups

1952	54.0	33.2	4.7	8.1
1956	51.1	32.7	5.3	10.9
1960	56.8	28.3	4.3	10.6
1964	54.4	27.2	7.4	10.9
1968	58.5	25.4	5.5	10.6
1972	54.7	23.8	8.5	12.9
1976	55.0	24.3	9.1	11.6
1980	59.7	28.3	5.2	6.9

General political philosophy

1952	65.1	20.9	8.8	5.2
1956	76.3	15.7	4.9	3.1
1960	68.1	15.9	9.5	6.5
1964	54.6	14.8	16.5	14.1
1968	54.2	19.3	13.7	12.7
1972	62.8	16.7	12.3	8.2
1976	63.6	17.8	10.9	7.7
1980	69.7	13.2	9.1	7.9

SOURCE: SRC/CPS National Election Studies.

Johnson's Great Society program produced a significant resurgence of party on domestic issues in 1968, but by 1972 Nixon's "imperial presidency" and the disarray of the Democrats pushed the relative salience of party on domestic policy to yet another new low. In addition, Nixon's strong personal handling of foreign policy and McGovern's extreme stance on Vietnam resulted in the largest four-year decline in the relative salience of parties versus candidates on foreign issues. Once again in 1976 we see some regression back to the previous state of affairs, probably because of the relative dearth of public knowledge about the issue stands of both Ford and Carter in that year. However, the most recent data from 1980 show a further continuation of the trend toward pure candidate orientation in the public's conceptualization of both domestic and foreign issues. The 1980 election focused primarily on the relative abilities of the candidates to handle successfully the problems of inflation, unemployment, and the hostage crisis in Iran,[16] and therefore it should not be surprising to find that the public came to view the issues in a more candidate-centered fashion than ever before.

Thus it seems clear that political leadership is one crucial variable in determining why the electorate has become more neutral toward the political parties. As presidential candidates have increasingly come to assume a much larger share of the spotlight on domestic and foreign policy, the parties have seen much of their base of support erode. A contest for the electorate's attention has taken place throughout the 1952–1980 period between presidential candidates and political parties, and a series of strong candidates have all contributed to the erosion of the electoral salience of parties. The likes and dislikes that citizens perceive for leaders on the issues are apparently not being translated into similar attitudes toward the parties.

Finally, in an attempt to advance, and further clarify, the argument that leadership is one of the key reasons behind the rise in neutrality, we can also examine responses concerning leaders on the *party* like/dislike questions. If the explanation for party decline is simply that candidates have become more salient, then one might expect that more people would be referring to leaders when asked about their likes and dislikes of the parties, even though other types of responses on the open-ended party questions have decreased. But if the decline is also due to the fact that the link between parties and candidates has been weakened, then it is probable that fewer people would be mentioning leaders when probed for their opinions about the parties, despite the fact that candidates have become increasingly salient to the electorate.

In working with these responses, one must be careful to compare years in which the leadership situations were as similar as possible; otherwise the results might simply be due to some exogenous factor such as whether the incumbent was running for reelection or not. The best set of comparisons that can be made are those between 1956 and 1972, when a popular incumbent was seeking reelection, and between 1964 and 1976, when recent midterm successors to the presidential office sought a term of their own.

These two comparisons support the hypothesis that the party-candidate link has indeed deteriorated. In 1956, 34.4 percent of the respondents mentioned a party figure as a reason for liking or disliking a party; only 19.0 percent did so in 1972. The comparable figures for 1964 and 1976 are

20.4 and 14.5 percent, respectively. The first comparison is particularly interesting, for Eisenhower was a far less partisan figure than Nixon. One plausible explanation could be Eisenhower's great personal popularity in 1956. Yet it is not merely positive responses about party leaders that were more prevalent in 1956; dislikes were more frequently mentioned as well. In fact, more people, when asked what they disliked about the Democratic Party, mentioned party leaders in 1956 than in 1972, even though Stevenson was a far more popular standard-bearer than McGovern. Regarding the incumbent party, 9.4 percent expressed some dislike of its leaders in 1956 compared to only 3.4 percent in 1972. Although most of the negative comments concerning the Republicans in 1956 were directed at Nixon rather than Eisenhower, it is somewhat unexpected that fewer people would give similar comments about him in 1972, when he was an incumbent president.

At least a partial answer to the question "Why the growing neutrality toward the parties?" seems to be that fewer people are translating their likes and dislikes about the candidates and the candidates' stands on specific issues into likes and dislikes about the parties. Thus the appearance of a major realigning issue—which is so often considered to be the best hope for reviving the parties— may not have any strengthening effect on partisanship in the electorate. The reason for party decline has not been that people no longer see any important differences between the parties. Indeed, the trend toward neutrality would have been even sharper if the frequency of comments concerning the general philosophies and group benefits offered by the parties had not remained fairly stable. Rather, the problem the parties face is that they are considered less relevant in solving the most important domestic and foreign policy issues of the day. In the voters' minds, the parties are losing their association with the candidates and the issues that the candidates claim to stand for. Therefore, major new issues that arise will probably not help the parties rebuild their base of support unless voters are convinced that the parties can serve a meaningful function that candidates alone cannot.

6
The Role of the Media

Thus far it has been argued that the decline of partisanship has involved a change in the public agenda from parties to candidates. Naturally, any time such an agenda change is found it must be considered what part the media has played—for its role in shaping the public agenda is well known.

The tremendous growth of the media has undoubtedly been one of the most important factors in reshaping the American electoral scene in recent years. Where once candidates for public office had to rely on mustering organizational strength to communicate with voters, it is now increasingly possible for them to establish direct contact through the media. As a result, what Robert Agranoff has labeled "the candidate-centered campaign" has come into prominence.[1] Once, a major theme of most campaigns involved stressing the candidate's party affiliation; now candidates often run campaigns that deemphasize party ties whenever possible. As Fiorina has written, "Candidates would have little incentive to operate campaigns independent of parties if there were no means to apprise the citizenry of their independence.

The media provide the means" (emphasis mine).[2] There is of course nothing inherent about the media which requires that campaigns be run independently of party; rather, the growth of the media has simply made this strategy far more feasible. Such a style of media campaigning reinforces attitudes about candidates but does little to reinforce partisan attitudes. As Frank Sorauf writes, "It is the candidate, not the party, who is 'sold.' The image transmitted by TV and the other media is of a person, not of the abstraction known as a political party."[3]

Newspaper and television reporting have in all likelihood also fostered the declining salience of political parties. Newspapers, which were once one of the prime reinforcers of partisanship, now take a largely independent line—especially in the everyday reporting of the news. As James Sundquist has noted, it is rare today to find a newspaper which endorses a straight party slate: "A self-respecting editor feels obliged to advise his readers to split their tickets."[4] And television coverage of politics virtually ignores parties, as acquaintance with personalities is much easier to convey through the visual media than knowledge about abstractions such as political parties.

Despite the frequent assertions in the literature of the media's contribution to the decline of partisanship, the evidence has remained almost entirely impressionistic. The goal of this chapter is to remedy this deficiency by first examining data that demonstrate the historical shift in the focus of election coverage from parties to candidates, and then analyzing the effects of candidate media advertising on the salience of partisan attitudes in the mass public.

A Content Analysis of Election Coverage

Are political parties in fact now receiving less coverage in election reporting, compared to candidates, than in the past? With the great number of media sources in the United States, attempting to reach a definitive empirical answer to this question would require resources far beyond those available for this inquiry. However, I sought to test this hypothesis on a limited basis by examining the content of election coverage between 1952 and 1980 in two major metropolitan newspapers and three national weekly news magazines. The two newspapers—the *Chicago Tribune* and the *Washington Post*—were selected randomly from a rather limited selection; no claim can be made for their being representative of the cross-section of newspapers around the country. The selection of the three weekly news magazines—*Newsweek, Time,* and *U.S. News and World Report*—was somewhat less arbitrary, as they constitute the only major national weekly news magazines published throughout this period.

The research design employed was to have students code a portion of the election coverage for each presidential election from 1952 to 1980, dividing up the workload so that each student coded roughly the same amount of material in each year.[5] All election-related stories in September and October were coded for each news source, totaling 10,115 stories in all over the course of eight elections. The major objective of the coding was to count the number of times political parties were mentioned by name in the stories and headlines compared to presidential candidates. In addition, on a more subjective level, coders were instructed to look for and count the number of substantive linkages between parties and candidates in the content of the stories.

Starting with the results from coding the stories, the data clearly indicate that media coverage of candidates has increasingly come to dominate that of parties in the newspapers and magazines selected for analysis.[6] Although the total number of campaign-related stories declined in this period, the actual number of mentions of presidential candidates per year stayed relatively stable. In contrast, the number of instances in which parties were mentioned by name in the stories fell precipitously. More theoretically important than the raw count of mentions, however, is the ratio between coverage of candidates versus that of parties, as this focuses attention squarely on the question of the *relative* degree to which the reading audience was exposed to candidates versus parties. Throughout the whole 1952–1980 period, mentions of candidates outnumbered those of parties, but as Figure 6.1 shows, the ratio increased from about two to one in the 1950s to roughly five to one by 1980. In short, it is clear that subscribers to these newspapers and magazines have over the years been increasingly exposed to a candidate-centered view of presidential campaigns.

A similar finding can be shown for the appearance of candidates and parties in the headlines of election coverage. A headline is an important barometer of what editors feel is most important in the news, as it is used to draw attention to a story and single out its key points. And as Figure 6.2 demonstrates, the editors for these news sources have increasingly come to believe that candidates are more newsworthy, and therefore more appropriate as headline material, than political parties. Given that there is much less material to code in headlines than in stories, it should not be surprising to find a somewhat less linear trend in the candidate/party ratio for the former. There is little doubt nevertheless that headline writers are much

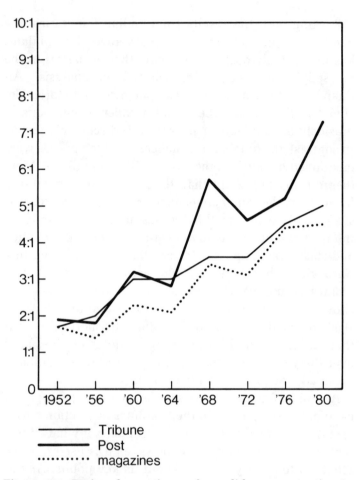

Figure 6.1 Ratio of mentions of candidates to parties in stories, 1952–1980

less inclined than in the past to place political parties in bold print, where even the most casual reader might take notice.

Beyond the straightforward counting of mentions of parties and candidates in election stories and headlines it

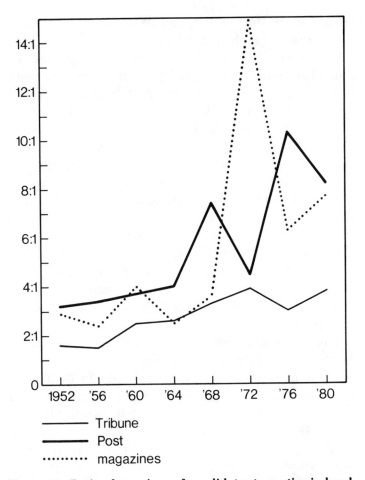

Figure 6.2   Ratio of mentions of candidates to parties in headlines, 1952–1980

is also important to examine some of the substance of election reporting. In particular, the data concerning the increased separation between public attitudes toward parties and candidates documented in the previous chapter would lead us to hypothesize that the party-candidate linkage is one theme that may be far less prevalent in election reporting than in the past.

Coders were thus instructed to count the number of instances in which presidential candidates were in some way tied to their party. This could be done in an election story by the reporter, by one of the candidates themselves, or by some other political figure. An example of the first kind of linkage would be a story reading, "Ronald Reagan campaigned in the Northeast yesterday expressing the usual Republican philosophy of free enterprise to traditional Republican constituencies." The second type would be exemplified by a quotation of Reagan saying, "Jimmy Carter favors the old Democratic beliefs of big spending and represents a party whose ideas have failed the test of time." (Note that in this case the linkage is the result of one candidate's linking his opponent to the opposition party.) And finally, if some other political figure was quoted as making such a statement (for instance, Truman in 1952 or Ford in 1980), then it was coded under the third type of substantive linkage.

The *total* number of linkages per year in each news source is displayed graphically in Figure 6.3, indicating a decline in magnitude of approximately two-thirds from 1952 to 1980.[7] If these linkages are broken down into the three categories described above, the trends are found to be remarkably similar. Candidates and other political figures are being quoted less often as making partisan statements and reporters are not invoking the theme of linkage between party and candidate as often as in the past. Whether all of this is due to changes in candidate behavior, or, alternatively, to changes in political reporting, is impossible to determine for certain. The degree to which this trend can be attributed to the reporters and editors is questionable, as it is difficult to say whether they are se-

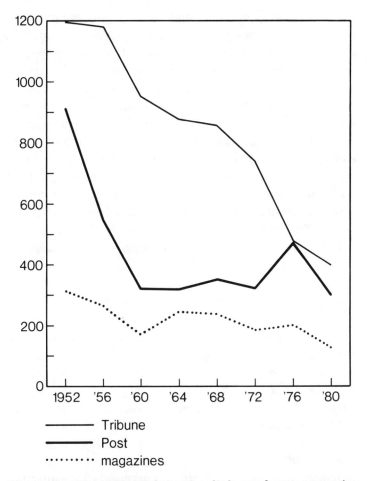

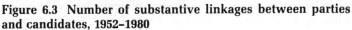

Figure 6.3 Number of substantive linkages between parties and candidates, 1952–1980

lectively reporting or mirroring the themes of the campaign. However, considering the sharpness of the decline, it seems unlikely that such linkages would be appearing so much less often in print if candidates were still emphasizing partisanship as frequently as in the past.

It has been found, then, that political parties have been increasingly eclipsed by, and separated from, presidential candidates in the election coverage of the two newspapers and three magazines for which data were collected. Of course, even presuming that these findings are representative of the pattern for the American print media as a whole, there is no direct evidence that such changes in election coverage have had any effect on attitudes in the electorate. The aggregate trends do match each other nicely, but left unanswered is the crucial question of whether people who are more exposed to a candidate-centered campaign in the media become less partisan as a result. The remainder of this chapter will examine the best available data on this relationship and the conditions that foster it.

The Data Base

Only uncontrolled media messages have been examined thus far. We will now turn to controlled media messages, for which data can be more easily linked to mass political attitudes. This inquiry will rely on information about seventy-eight campaigns for the House of Representatives in 1978. Data about media expenditures and other aspects of the campaign were gathered by Michael Traugott and Edie Goldenberg in their survey of Democratic and Republican congressional campaign managers.[8] Because the interviews with the campaign managers were conducted in the same districts as the 1978 CPS Election Study, it is possible to investigate whether the districts with heavy media campaigns are also those where the saliency of political parties in the electorate is lowest.

Such a cross-sectional correlation does not, however,

provide evidence from which to infer a definitive causal relationship. In fact, the causality probably operates to some degree in both directions, with reliance on the media weakening partisan attitudes in the electorate and with low levels of partisanship increasing the probability of waging a more candidate-centered media campaign. However, regardless of the causality underlying the relationship, its existence indicates that the media are playing a role in the process of transforming the public's focus on politics from parties to candidates.

The Decline of Partisanship in Congressional Elections

The use of congressional-year data represents a significant departure from the presidential orientation of the rest of this work. Thus a brief look at partisanship in congressional elections may be helpful at this point.

For many years it was a point of conventional wisdom that congressional elections are primarily partisan affairs in which voters cast their ballots for the candidate of their party, with little or no knowledge of the candidates.[9] To be sure, some deviations from the normal vote were to be expected, but by and large national forces, rather than individual candidates, were thought to be at the root of such deviations.[10] However, over the last several years many researchers have come to question whether such an interpretation of congressional elections remains valid. The percentage of party-line votes cast in congressional elections has fallen steadily from 84 percent in 1958 to only 69 percent in 1978. In fact, in 1976 more votes were actually cast according to party lines in the presidential race than for the House.[11] That parties are far less important to the electorate than in the past during congressional elections can be shown clearly by comparing the responses to the open-ended questions in the two congressional years for which such data are available. In 1958 only 23.7 percent of the electorate could be classified as neutral toward both parties, compared to 45.7 percent in 1978. Interestingly, the decline in salience from the presidential to congressional year is much steeper in the latter period, indicating that these attitudes are now less likely to endure to the off-year as well as being less stable from one presidential election to the next (see Chapter 2).

Unfortunately, like/dislike questions concerning congressional candidates were asked only in 1978, but it seems likely that if there were comparable data for 1958 the trend would show a greater degree of saliency. As Thomas Mann has written, "Increasingly, congressmen are responsible for their own margins of victory or defeat, and the electoral constraints they face are defined largely in their individual districts."[12] Through the media, congressional candidates now have the capability of making themselves far more visible than in the past, and to the degree that their campaigns are run independently of party one would expect a decline in the saliency and intensity of partisan attitudes in the electorate.

Media Expenditures and Partisan Attitudes

In order to test this hypothesis, we will employ two different measures for which comparable indices can be constructed concerning attitudes about both parties and candidates. The first involves simply counting the number of responses to the like/dislike questions in order to create interval level salience measures for purposes of correlational analysis. The second measure makes use of the intensity of respondents' feeling thermometer ratings precisely along the same lines of distance from the neutral point as described in Chapter 4.

For the purposes of this analysis, campaigns are best specified as interactive events in which voters can learn about specific candidates and parties from the efforts of both sides. For example, the salience of the Democratic Party may be just as much due to the negative advertising undertaken by the Republicans as the positive appeals by the Democrats. Therefore, the candidate and party salience and intensity measures are calculated on the basis of respondents' attitudes in each district toward both the Democrats and Republicans. Similarly, the major independent variable of this analysis, the amount of money spent on media advertising,[13] involves adding together what the two campaign managers estimated their campaign expenses to be in this area.

Table 6.1 shows the relationship between the amount of money spent in the campaign on media (both mass media and other media, such as billboards and buttons) and candidate and party salience and intensity. It is hardly sur-

Table 6.1 Correlations between advertising/media expenses and party and candidate salience and intensity measures

	Candidates	Parties	
Feeling thermometers[a]	.31	−.19	(n = 78)
Likes/dislikes[b]	.39	−.12	(n = 78)

a. This measure represents the average distance from 50 degrees which respondents in each district rate the candidates or parties.

b. This measure represents the mean number of likes and dislikes expressed by the respondents in each district.

SOURCE: 1978 CPS National Election Study and Traugott-Goldenberg Study of Campaign Managers.

prising to find that as the two candidates advertise more they become more salient to the general public—after all, that is part of the purpose of their doing so. However, it is not self-evident that a higher level of campaign media expenses should be associated with a lower degree of party salience in the electorate, as is shown by the two negative correlations in Table 6.1. If partisanship were stressed in campaigns, one might expect both sets of correlations to be positive. But apparently the effect of candidates' media advertising is solely the projection of candidate images, and not that of party images. Although the negative correlations between media expenses and partisanship are not of great magnitude, the cumulative effect of such a pattern over time could possibly account for a significant portion of the long-term trend.[14]

The Mediating Effect of Local Party Organizations

It should not be assumed, however, that media advertising has the same degree of effect on partisan attitudes under all conditions, for the media are used differently in some circumstances than in others. One of the factors that may affect the relationship between media advertising and partisanship is the strength of the local party organizations in the district. Although party machines capable of single-handedly electing candidates have virtually disappeared, party organizations nevertheless still play a significant role in determining the electoral outcome in many areas of the country. Of all the campaign managers who were interviewed in 1978, 12 percent said that they thought their party organization would be very important in determining the outcome of the general election for Congress in their district, 15 percent stated it was quite important, 30 percent fairly important, 29 percent not very important, and 14 percent stated that it was not at all important.[15]

Because the level of analysis for this portion of analysis is the congressional district, the responses from both managers in each race were combined in order to create a variable measuring the importance of local party organizations. In twenty-six districts both managers stated that the party organization would be at least fairly important in determining the electoral outcome; in thirty-five others, either both managers said their organization was not important or else one manager said it was only fairly important and the other said it was not important. (The seventeen cases where one manager said the organization was very or quite important and the opponent said it was not important have been excluded from this section of analysis.)

Table 6.2 demonstrates that when the party organizations are judged to be important in influencing the vote, the relationship between media expenses and candidate and party salience and intensity are quite different from when the organizations are not perceived as important. With both the feeling thermometers and the like/dislike measures, correlations between media expenditures and partisanship are much more negative in districts where the organizations are unimportant than where they are important. It may be that candidates simply do not have any reason to orient their media strategy toward any sort of partisan appeal when the organization is not important, for such tactics are not likely to be beneficial to them.

That party organizations do have the potential to be of substantial aid to candidates, however, is indirectly indicated by the much lower correlations between media ex-

Table 6.2 Correlations between salience and intensity measures and media expenses by strength of local party organizations

	Candidates	Parties	
Feeling thermometers			
Party organizations important	.18	−.09	(n = 26)
Party organizations not important	.50	−.42	(n = 35)
Like/dislikes			
Party organizations important	.26	−.02	(n = 26)
Party organizations not important	.64	−.21	(n = 35)

SOURCE: 1978 CPS National Election Study and Traugott-Goldenberg Study of Campaign Managers.

penditures and the candidate salience and intensity measures where the organizations are judged by the managers to be important. It is unlikely that money spent on the media in these districts is less effective. Rather, it is more plausible that where party organizations are strong, the amount of money spent on the media will have less effect on the projection of candidate images because it represents a much smaller proportion of the total communications from the candidates to the voters. In these areas, other activities—such as canvassing by the organizations—may be substantially responsible for levels of candidate salience, and this may reduce the correlations with the level of media advertising.

To summarize briefly, the strength of the local party organization is an important intervening variable in the relationship between media expenditures and the party and candidate salience and intensity measures. Where the parties are not thought by campaign managers to be important in determining the outcome, the degree of media advertising is more negatively related to party salience and intensity and more positively related to candidate salience and intensity.

Mass Media versus Other Media

All media are not alike. Thus far, a variety of types of media expenses—from TV ads to billboards—have been lumped together to represent all the efforts of the candidates to put themselves in touch with the voters. Fortunately, the managers were also asked to estimate how they allocated their advertising/media budgets. The most important distinction that can be made between types of media expenses is that between mass media (TV, radio, and newspapers) and more indirect media (campaign literature, buttons, billboards, and so on). The latter are obviously more dependent on backing from a strong organization, as such advertising requires someone to pass out the literature and buttons and put up the yard signs. In contrast, money can easily buy all the skills necessary to make mass media advertisements effective.

One would expect, therefore, that in districts where the party organizations are important, a greater percentage of campaign advertising will be devoted to media other than TV, radio, or newspapers. While campaign strategies are not always based entirely on rational considerations, it would be surprising not to find that campaigns make more use of these media when it is more feasible and productive to do so. Indeed, it is found that in districts where the local party organizations are not important candidates allocate roughly 20 percent more of their budget to the mass media than in districts where the organizations are perceived to be strong—73 versus 54 percent.

The consequences of this difference are illustrated in Table 6.3. Evidently, mass media advertising is negatively related to partisanship regardless of whether or not the local party organizations are important—perhaps because the mass media orient advertising toward the projection of candidate images rather than party images. Even if a congressional candidate should go out of his or her way to attempt to portray a partisan image through the mass media, the crucial fact is that the voters are looking at, listening to, and reading about the candidates. The partisanship measures, however, show a different pattern in areas with strong organizations compared to those with weak organizations. Where the party organizations are not important, spending on both types of media is negatively related to party saliency and intensity, but in areas with strong party organizations only the correlation with mass media expenditures is negative. The reason for this difference probably has to do with the way these other types of media advertising are disseminated. It is easy to see how partisanship might suffer if autonomous candidate-centered organizations are completely responsible for distributing this material, but when party organizations participate in passing out leaflets and other material one should not expect to find such an effect.

One might even expect to find a strong positive correlation under the latter circumstance. However, American local party organizations are usually not very active and haven't been for decades. For example, Samuel Eldersveld found that in Detroit in 1956 that parties were far

Table 6.3 Correlations between salience and intensity measures and amount of mass and other media expenses by strength of local party organizations

	Candidates		Parties	
	Feeling thermometers	Likes/ dislikes	Feeling thermometers	Likes/ dislikes
Party organizations important				
Mass media	.09	.27	−.27	−.22
Other media	.00	−.06	.04	−.03
				(n = 26)
Party organizations not important				
Mass media	.46	.61	−.37	−.15
Other media	.29	.42	−.49	−.12
				(n = 35)

Source: 1978 CPS National Election Study and Traugott-Goldenberg Study of Campaign Managers.

from "monolithic efficiency structures."[16] Less than one-fifth of the local organizations could be classified as operating near the peak of their potential performance on organizational tasks, according to Eldersveld. Similarly, Charles Clapp found that congressional participants in a 1958 Brookings roundtable discussion felt that party organizations were ineffective in providing support. As one Congressman stated, "If we depended on the party organization to get elected, none of us would be here."[17]

In sum, weak as they may be elsewhere, in districts where party organizations are considered to be unimportant by the campaign managers, media expenditures are much more negatively related to party salience and intensity for two reasons. First, where the organizations are most important, a smaller percentage of the candidate's media budget is allocated to the mass media, and the mass media are particularly conducive to projecting candidate rather than party images. Second, when party organizations are important, the amount of money spent on other types of media is not negatively correlated with party salience, for the organization participates at least to some degree in these activities.

However, the potential of local parties to reverse the decline of partisan attitudes in the electorate should not be exaggerated. Even if local parties were to become better organized and effective in the near future, there is little they could do to prevent the probable increase in direct candidate appeals through the mass media. Furthermore, it is likely that local parties will become even more dispensable to candidates as political action committees (PACs) continue to multiply and provide services that previously were often provided by the parties.

The Role of PAC Campaign Contributions

The post-Watergate campaign finance reforms have had a major effect on how political campaigns are run in the United States. One of the most notable changes involves the rapid growth of PACs, each of which represents a specific interest group rather than the aggregation of groups that a party represents. PAC contributions to congressional campaigns have grown steadily in recent years. In 1978 PAC contributions amounted to one-quarter of the funds raised by congressional candidates compared to only 7 percent for parties.[18] Some observers, such as Fred Wertheimer of Common Cause, have even speculated that soon PACs will virtually dominate congressional campaigns.

In the context of this chapter the growth of PACs is important for two reasons. First, PACs threaten to further displace the party organizations as a useful tool for political candidates. Not only are they contributing significant amounts of money to campaigns, they are also rapidly learning how to aid candidates in organizational tasks. Second, PAC money is interested money and therefore bound to have an influence on how campaigns are conducted. It is increasingly difficult for candidates to make broad partisan appeals when their campaign treasuries become dependent on pleasing a variety of special interests.

The first hypothesis stated above—that PACs threaten to further displace the party organizations—is clearly supported by the data. Dividing districts into roughly equal thirds according to the percentage of campaign expenditures contributed by PACs reveals that the likelihood of the manager responding that the party organization was important declines from 56, to 35, to 31 per-cent as PAC contributions increase. Because of the cross-sectional nature of the data, however, the causality of this relationship must remain somewhat uncertain. In part, it may be due to a rational calculation on the part of the PACs concerning where their money would most likely be influential. However, from a dynamic perspec-tive it seems inevitable that as PAC contributions come to make up a larger percentage of campaign budgets, other factors such as local party organizations will become less important to the candidates.

In addition, as hypothesized above, PAC contributions are also likely to influence the nature of communication messages stressed by campaigns. Thus the proportion of money contributed by PACs should have an effect on the relationship between partisanship and campaign media expenditures. As demonstrated in Table 6.4, the level of media expenditures is far more negatively correlated with the partisanship measures in districts where PACs con-tributed most heavily than in those where PACS had least importance. Furthermore, this difference is independent of the strength of local party organizations, as indicated by the partial correlation coefficients.

The results presented in this chapter confirm the fre-quent assertion of media research that although media appeals may not be able to tell citizens what to think, they can profoundly influence what people think *about*. One of the most astute political cartoons concerning the media in recent years pictures a young boy asking his father, "Dad, if a tree falls in the forest, and the media aren't there to cover it, has the tree really fallen?"[19] Political parties do still exist despite their neglect by the media, but the gen-

Table 6.4 Correlations between advertising/media expenses and salience and intensity measures by percentage of expenditures contributed by PACs

	Candidates	Parties	
Feeling thermometers			
Low (0–16%)	.41 (.43)[a]	.02 (−.02)	(n = 19)[b]
Medium (17–33%)	.39 (.39)	.08 (−.14)	(n = 23)
High (over 33%)	.40 (.60)	−.35 (−.44)	(n = 17)
Likes/dislikes			
Low (0–16%)	.41 (.53)	−.12 (−.03)	(n = 19)
Medium (17–33%)	.34 (.44)	−.20 (−.30)	(n = 23)
High (over 33%)	.65 (.79)	−.25 (−.31)	(n = 17)

a. Correlations in parentheses represent partial correlations controlling for whether the party organizations in the district are judged to be important by the managers.

b. Case numbers are slightly less for the partial correlations because some districts cannot be categorized as having either strong or weak organizations.

SOURCE: 1978 CPS National Election Study and Traugott-Goldenberg Study of Campaign Managers.

eral emphasis of media campaigns on candidates rather than parties has served to make them less institutionally relevant and salient to the mass public.

The ultimate question to consider is whether such changes have been beneficial to the functioning of American democracy. One might argue that the shift in electoral salience should foster better representation as the electorate becomes more informed about congressional candidates. However, what voters know about the candidates on this level apparently has little to do with issues. Only 14 percent of the likes and dislikes expressed about the candidates for Congress in 1978 could be said to be references about matters of public policy, compared to 47 percent of the responses about political parties. As Miller and Stokes concluded in their classic study of constituency influence in Congress during the late 1950s, the party symbol performs a crucial linkage in the representation process because "the constituency can infer the candidates' position with more than random accuracy even though what the constituency has learned directly about these stands is almost nothing."[20] With parties becoming increasingly less likely to perform this linkage and without voter knowledge of congressional candidates' positions, the chances for faithful representation are clearly reduced.

7
Demographic Trends

The previous two chapters have documented the effects of the political factors of leadership and the media on the decline in the salience of party. Whenever a secular trend in political behavior is discovered, however, long-term demographic changes must always be considered as a possible cause. Over a period of several decades there will necessarily be a tremendous amount of population replacement, and new entrants into the electorate may be quite different from their elders demographically in such a way that their political attitudes differ as well. Under such a scenario, changes in the composition of the electorate, rather than changes among those already in the electorate, may be primarily responsible for the decline of partisanship. One could thus readily interpret the decline as something that should not have been unexpected, given the nature of recent demographic shifts. Therefore, if it can be shown that nonpolitical, demographic factors have *not* been responsible for the decline of partisanship, then the argument in favor of real-world changes in the conduct of American politics will be further strengthened.

Two basic changes in the composition of the electorate

stand out as the most plausible demographic factors for the decline of partisanship. First, the level of formal education has risen steadily in the electorate over the last several decades, and hence voters may now be better prepared to make political judgments without the aid of partisan cues. Second, there is the possibility that the decline may be limited to the influx of new voters into the electorate, whose generation has experienced a fundamentally different socialization process from that of previous generations. Both of these potential explanations will be examined in this chapter.

Education

As Philip Converse has remarked, the growth of higher education is probably the most massive social change to be found in the SRC/CPS election study time series.[1] In 1952 only 15 percent of the population had received some college education and the training of 41 percent was limited to no more than grade school. By 1980 the educational balance had flipped to the point where 37 percent had attended college while only 12 percent had just a grade school education.

The thesis that better-educated voters should have a weaker sense of partisanship can be found in numerous sources in the academic literature. For example, Everett Carll Ladd and Charles D. Hadley write that one main effect of the explosion of higher education "has been to expand dramatically the proportion of the population which feels no need for parties as active intermediaries in the voting decision."[2] Or as Frank Sorauf writes, party loyalty makes demands that the educated citizen is less willing to accommodate. These more educated voters are too well informed politically to "divide the political world into two simple categories, ours and theirs," according to Sorauf.[3] In sum, the theoretical basis for relating changes in education to the erosion of partisanship in the electorate depends quite heavily on a rationalistic view of the partisanship concept. According to this perspective, partisanship is primarily a device by which uninformed and uninvolved voters can avoid dealing with the complexities of the political world.

Despite the tremendous growth of higher education, however, there is little evidence that the electorate is much more involved in, or informed about, politics than in the 1950s. There has been an increase in several forms of political participation, such as letter writing to public officials, but these have been fairly slight in magnitude.[4] Furthermore, the most important form of participation— voting—has actually declined. As for the electorate's level of political sophistication, there has been a rise of about 14 percent in the proportion of the population that conceptualizes politics in abstract ideological terms,[5] but on specific issues people were no more likely to hold stable attitudes in the 1950s than in the 1970s.[6] And finally, on the most basic level, the public still remains strikingly uninformed about many political events and issues. For example, only 15 percent of those interviewed after the 1980 election could correctly identify which party had won the most seats in the House of Representatives and only 22 percent knew that Ronald Reagan advocated a 30 percent cut in federal income taxes.

Thus, on close examination, the hypothesized relationship between the growth of education and the decline of partisanship appears quite weak theoretically. If greater education has not produced a much more involved and informed electorate, then why should it have played any role in the weakening of partisanship? Indeed, Figures 7.1–7.4 demonstrate that the decline of partisanship has been nearly identical across all educational levels.

First, on strength of party identification we see that

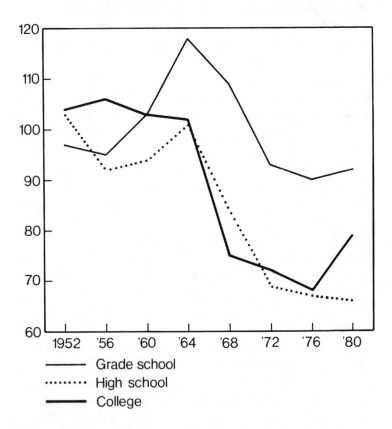

Figure 7.1 Strength of party identification by level of education, 1952–1980
Note: See Table 4.3 for a description of the strength of party identification index used in this figure.
Source: SRC/CPS National Election Studies.

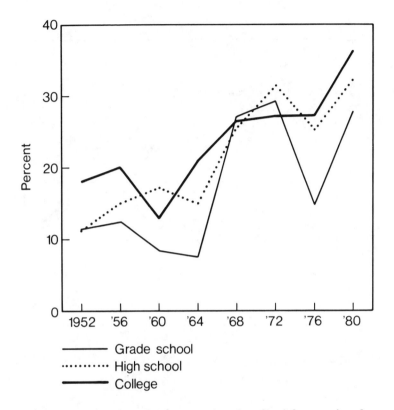

Figure 7.2   Presidential-congressional split-ticket voting by level of education, 1952–1980
Source: SRC/CPS National Election Studies.

higher education has not always been synonymous with the greatest sense of independence (see Figure 7.1). In fact, from 1952 to 1960 college-educated citizens actually displayed the highest level of party identification, and only in 1968 were they lowest on the index. It is true that since 1964 grade school-educated respondents have consistently been the most strongly partisan, but this is

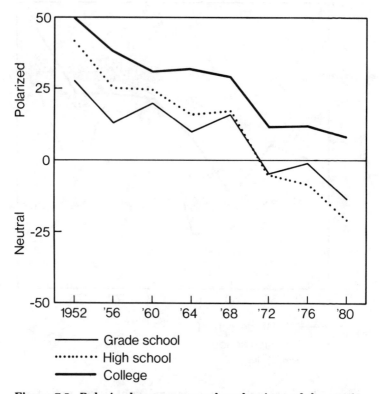

Figure 7.3   Polarized versus neutral evaluations of the parties by level of education, 1952–1980

Note: Figure entries represent the proportion of respondents positive toward one party and negative toward the other on the like/dislike questions minus the proportion neutral toward both parties.

Source: SRC/CPS National Election Studies.

largely a spurious relationship because older people have come to be greatly overrepresented among those with only a grade school education.[7] What is important about Figure 7.1 is that it shows that the decline in strength of party identification has been roughly parallel from one education bracket to another. Similarly, from the data displayed in Figure 7.2 we can draw much the same conclusions regarding split-ticket voting. The static relationship between education and splitting one's ticket has varied considerably over the years, indicating that such behavior is by no means restricted only to better educated voters, and dynamically the increase is roughly equal in each of the three categories of educational training.

Figures 7.3 and 7.4, which display data from the like/dislike and feeling thermometer questions discussed in Chapter 6, also show similar patterns of decline across

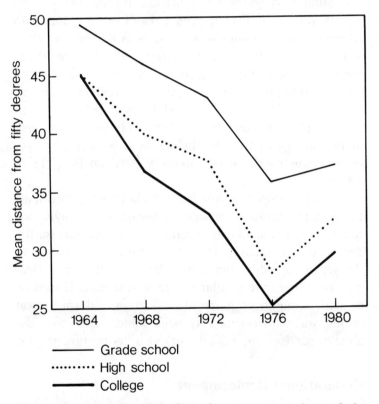

Figure 7.4 Intensity of feeling thermometer ratings of the parties by level of education, 1964–1980
Source: SRC/CPS National Election Studies.

educational groups. In both cases, however, one can also discern a consistent difference by education in attitudes toward the parties that sheds some light on the nature of the difference between the two measures. On the like/dislike probes the responses of those who have had some college education are always the most skewed toward polarized rather than neutral views of the parties (see Figure 7.3). This is quite likely due to the greater ability to articulate one's feelings that comes with a higher education. College-educated citizens are less likely to be classified as neutral simply as a result of an inability to respond to the open-ended questions. A higher education also contributes to a more moderate view of the world in which extreme attitudes become tempered.[8] Thus, when we turn to the intensity of respondents' feeling thermometer ratings of the parties, the relationship between partisan attitudes and education is found to be just the reverse of the pattern of the like/dislike data, with the college-educated being the least intensely partisan (see Figure 7.4).

These two opposing relationships between partisan attitudes and education provide further theoretical evidence that the growth of education cannot be responsible for the decline of partisanship. Holding everything else constant, the growth of education should have resulted in contradictory rather than similar patterns over time. However, as with strength of party identification and split-ticket voting, there have evidently been factors causing a decline in partisanship equally among all education groups.

Generational Replacement

One such possible factor is another demographic trend—generational replacement. Indeed, generational differences have been perhaps the most widely discussed and thoroughly investigated reason for the decline of parties in the electorate. Thus, given that we can rely heavily on other sources, our empirical treatment of this subject need not be as detailed as with education.

The evidence clearly shows that the decline in strength of party identification has come more from new entrants to the political system than from those who have abandoned already established ties. Arthur Miller and Warren Miller outline three age-related factors that have contributed to the decline of party identification. First, young nonpartisans have replaced older partisans; second, each new entering cohort has been less partisan; and finally, although there has been less change among those already in the electorate than among new voters, the former group has also declined somewhat in party strength.[9]

Left unanswered in this discussion is the key question of what has caused new entrants into the electorate to be so much weaker in party identification than their parents were at the same age. Paul Allen Beck's socialization theory of realignment provides an intriguing possible explanation.[10] Beck argues that the periodicity with which realignments have occurred throughout U.S. history has been a function of cyclical changes in the partisan socialization process. According to this theory, after a realignment occurs parents will be very conscious of the issues on which the new alignment has turned and will strongly transmit their partisan attachments to their offspring. These children of realignment, however, will be less successful in passing their party identification on to the next generation, because by this time the realigning issues will have faded as matters of serious political concern. As a result, the entrance of this less partisan generation into the electorate will contribute to a process of dealignment.

In addition, as a large, unmobilized block of voters, this generation also represents the potential for the next realignment on the basis of new issues.

Given that the last realignment occurred in the mid-1930s, Beck's theory nicely predicts the timing and generational nature of the decline in strength of party identification. It does not, however, fit quite so well with the more secular aspects of the decline of parties in the electorate. For example, although party identification has not eroded substantially among older cohorts, these voters have nevertheless followed the general trend toward split-ticket voting. As Nie et al. conclude, "The rise of split ticket voting appears to be more a function of the pressures of the period than the generation of the voter."[11]

If the partisan behavior patterns of older and younger voters have followed the same tendencies, then the fact that older voters have retained their partisan labels may be of little political significance—the identification may still be present but it may well mean much less to these citizens than in the past. Turning to the data from the like/dislike questions and feeling thermometers, it is clear that such is in fact the case. Figure 7.5 shows that all cohorts have moved toward a neutral evaluation of the parties, and Figure 7.6 shows that each has come to rate the parties with far less intensity on the feeling thermometers. Thus it is apparent that the generational nature of the decline in strength of party identification has been the exception rather than the rule. Older generations may have largely held on to their partisan labels, which were acquired during a period when the parties were more meaningful to voters than they are now, but the labels no longer have the importance they once had for these cohorts.

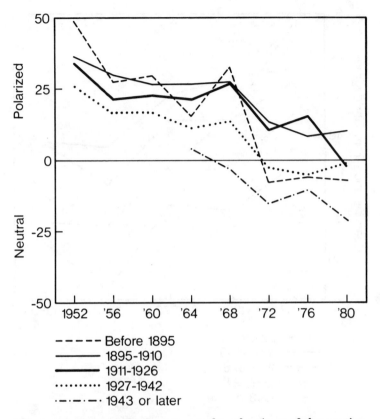

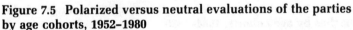

Figure 7.5 Polarized versus neutral evaluations of the parties by age cohorts, 1952–1980
Note: See Figure 7.3 for a description of the index used in this figure.
Source: SRC/CPS National Election Studies.

The findings presented in this chapter have demonstrated that neither education nor generational replacement has played a major role in the decline of political partisanship. These negative results make it evident that long-term factors involving changes in the character of

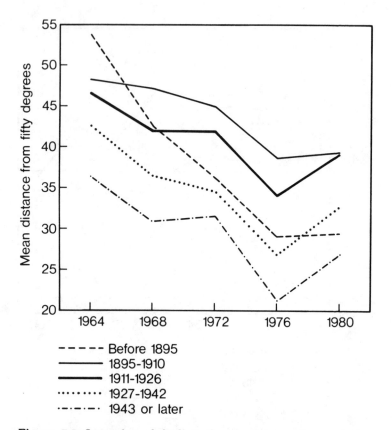

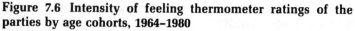

Figure 7.6 Intensity of feeling thermometer ratings of the parties by age cohorts, 1964–1980
Source: SRC/CPS National Election Studies.

American politics have caused people of all ages and all education brackets to change in their attitudes toward the parties. The political explanations for the decline of partisanship fit the data far better than the sociological explanations examined in this chapter.

8
The Public as an Echo Chamber

In his last book, *The Responsible Electorate*, V. O. Key outlined a basic theory of political behavior that came frequently to mind as I wrote this book. According to Key, "The voice of the people is but an echo chamber. The output of an echo chamber bears an inevitable and invariable relation to the input. As candidates and parties clamor for attention and vie for popular support, the people's verdict can be no more than a selective reflection from among the alternatives and outlooks presented to them."[1] The explanation for party decline in the electorate that has been argued in this book squares nicely with Key's echo chamber analogy.

The public did not decide all of a sudden that parties were bankrupt political institutions and mandate their decline. Rather, voters reacted gradually over the last quarter of a century to the way in which politics was presented to them. Political parties themselves became less institutionally relevant and the public adjusted their views of them accordingly. As party leaders have come to act more and more on their own initiative and to communicate with voters directly through the media, the public has increasingly come to see the crucial short-term domestic and foreign issues only in terms of the candidates. It is candidates rather than parties that are now viewed as being responsible for solving, or failing to solve, our current political problems. Therefore, the parties are receiving much less credit or blame for political outcomes than they did several decades ago. Despite the decay in public confidence in American political institutions in recent years, people have not turned sharply negative toward the parties. Instead they have come to see political parties as less relevant to what goes on in the everyday world of politics, and hence have become far more neutral toward them.

If the answer to the phenomenon of party decline in the electorate can in fact be found in the real world of elite political maneuvering, one might question why it is necessary to analyze mass survey data. My reply would be that although public opinion acts something like an echo chamber, without survey data one can never be sure just *what* people are reacting to. After all, there have been major political catastrophes (Vietnam, Watergate, economic recessions) for both parties in recent years, which could quite reasonably have led many voters to become negative toward both. Yet the change in the public's attitudes about the parties has been shaped not so much by specific political events as by how the events have been handled by leaders and presented by the media.

In order to reinvigorate political partisanship in the future, then, the public must be convinced that political parties perform a useful function in the American political process. The challenge that the parties face is not merely to espouse programs with popular appeal, but also to demonstrate that they play a crucial political role—

from the recruitment of leaders to the implementation of policies. If the echo chamber analogy is correct, then it is reasonable to assume that if leaders begin once again to act as partisans and be presented by the media as such, the decline of partisanship in the electorate can potentially be reversed.

The need for such a revitalization is hardly a new theme. Over thirty years ago a committee of distinguished political scientists concluded that our party system was functioning poorly in sustaining well-considered programs and mobilizing public support for them.[2] Numerous recommendations were compiled, all of which the scholars believed would facilitate a more responsible and effective party system—one that would be accountable to the public and able to deal with the problems of modern government.

These suggestions became an instant source of controversy and were justifiably criticized for their unrealistic call for more disciplined, programmatic, and ideologically distinctive parties in a political culture in which interests are too diverse to be expressed in the centralized fashion outlined in the recommendations.[3] Despite this critical flaw, however, what remains the central problem of the American party system was illuminated—namely, the relevance of political parties in solving governmental problems: "The party in power has a responsibility, broadly defined, for the general management of the government, for its manner of getting results achieved, for the consequences of inaction as well as action, for the intended and unintended outcome of its conduct of public affairs, for all that it plans to do, for all that it might have foreseen, for the leadership it provides, for the acts of all its agents, and for what it says as well as for what it does."[4] The sense of these scholars in 1950 that the parties were not adequately meeting their responsibilities led them to send out an alarm that a serious problem existed; the fact that parties are now even less capable of meeting these responsibilities is reflected in the survey data results presented in this book.

The skeptic might examine the long history of concern with the future of American political parties and conclude that some have cried wolf at least once too often. After all, over three decades later the two parties still remain intact in the world's oldest surviving party system. There seems to be no danger that the parties will suddenly vanish from the scene and leave catastrophic political and social chaos in their wake. The "party" is far from over, as Samuel Eldersveld has recently concluded.[5]

But although parties have not disintegrated they have clearly declined in relevance, and the consequences have been significant. In 1950 the scholars foresaw several dangers if no action was taken to make the party system more responsible. Their warnings seem eerily prophetic over three decades later; their fears have turned into our present-day realities. Indeed, examining what they saw as the dangers of a weakened party system illuminates some of our current problems.

A major fear was that if the parties could not develop comprehensive programs that could be successfully implemented, voter frustration might set in motion more extreme tendencies of both the left and the right, leading to a deep political cleavage "to which neither our political institutions nor our civic habits are adapted."[6] This fear has been at least partially realized in the turmoil of the 1960s and the development of strident single-issue groups. Parties once channeled political conflict and kept policy differences within reasonable bounds. One result of the decline of partisanship is that we now have a system that is capable of expressing a wide diversity of viewpoints but is rather poor at aggregating them. With parties increasingly less able to resolve these conflicts, the tone of American politics is becoming more negative and bitter, and policy compromises are much harder to come by.

A second possible consequence mentioned was the danger of overextending the presidency. As the only branch of government capable of leadership direction and unity of action, the presidency is the logical institution to expect the unmet responsibilities of the parties to fall upon. The problem with placing such expectations on the President is that "either his party becomes a flock of sheep or the party falls apart. In effect this concept of the presidency disposes of the party system by making the President reach directly for the support of a majority of votes. It favors a President who exploits skillfully the arts of demagoguery, who uses the whole country as his political backyard, and who does not mind turning into the embodiment of personal government."[7]

A generation before them, these political scientists speculated, such a prospect would have been dismissed as "fantastic." Today it is part of the modern presidency. Major policy proposals are presented to the public first and foremost as *presidential* programs. The economic program of the current administration, for example, is widely referred to not as Republican economics but as "Reaganomics." Of course it is members of the press rather than the president who have pinned this label on the program. However, as shown in Chapter 6, such press concentration on the president and presidential candidates has increasingly become the norm. It is no wonder that within such a political context the American public has become increasingly indifferent to the parties.

In 1950 just such a prospect was foreseen if party accountability were not restored. That the public might "turn its back upon the two parties" was a real possibility, and was in fact already beginning to occur: "Present conditions are a great incentive for the voters to dispose of the parties as intermediaries between themselves and the government. In a way, a sizeable body of the electorate has shifted from hopeful interest in the parties to the opposite attitude. This mass of voters sees itself as the President's or his opponent's direct electoral support."[8] Over three decades later this statement is now even more true.

Partisanship once provided the American electorate with a sense of continuity and stability. With its decline many citizens have been set adrift without an anchor in a political world full of strong eddies and currents. As a result, some no longer vote;[9] others are swept first one way and then another by the currents, causing the much talked-about rise of political volatility. Throughout the 1980 campaign political commentators frequently remarked on the high degree of changeability in voter preferences. One pointed indication of this volatility is the large percentage of voters who waited until very near the end of the campaign before they decided how to vote. In *The American Voter,* Campbell and his colleagues noted that most voters in 1952 and 1956 had made up their minds by the time of the nominating conventions, indicating "that the psychological forces guiding behavior arise before the campaign opens."[10] In 1980, however, half of the voters interviewed stated that they had made their decisions during the campaign, and an unprecedented 9 percent waited *until election day* to make up their minds (only 2 percent did so in each of the Eisenhower-Stevenson contests).

What was most striking about the last-minute decision-making in the 1980 campaign was the suddenness with which a virtually even race turned into a landslide victory for Ronald Reagan. As might be expected, given their lack of partisan direction, those who were neutral toward both parties on the like/dislike questions accounted for a large proportion (47.8 percent) of the undecided voters in the CPS preelection survey. Furthermore, they, much more than any other group of undecided voters, were swayed toward Reagan—casting an astounding 70.3 percent of their votes for him compared to 18.9 percent for Carter and 11.8 percent for Anderson. This is not to say that these voters alone accounted for the last-minute shift, but clearly it does indicate their great potential for volatile political behavior.

In conclusion, party coalitions in the United States have undergone a series of processes of decay over the last three decades, increasing the possibilities of *both* short-term and long-term change in the near future. With the weakening of the public's images of the parties, it is no wonder that volatility has become the new catchword of American politics. As the long-term forces that serve to anchor electoral behavior decline, the potential increases for large oscillations in the vote because of short-term issue and candidate factors. Furthermore, given that there is less of what V. O. Key called a "standing decision" for people to return to, there is also an increased potential for the translation of short-term forces into long-term ones. Such a process, however, will require that the issues and candidates responsible for the short-term changes become firmly linked with public images of the parties. When and if that happens, a new era of American electoral politics will have begun.

9

The Elections of 1984 and 1988: Realignment without Revitalization

The 1988 presidential election campaign illustrated many of the negative side effects of the decline of American political parties. Never in recent memory has a campaign been so widely criticized for being both overly bitter and devoid of substantive issues. The *Washington Post* spoke for many in the media when it declined to endorse either candidate, stating: "This has been a terrible campaign, a national disappointment."[1] As for the voters, a *New York Times*/CBS News post-election poll revealed that 68 percent thought the 1988 campaign had been more negative than campaigns of the past, compared with just 5 percent who felt it had been more positive.

Much ink has been spilled over why the campaign was conducted so harshly. Part of the explanation of course lies with the candidates themselves, their managers, and the absence of an incumbent running for reelection. A more overarching structural explanation, though, stems from the decline of parties as vote-mobilizing organizations. When party identification predetermined most voters' choices, candidates had little incentive to get down in the mud in an attempt to rip their opponent to shreds. Strong partisans would see their party's candidates in a favorable light no matter what the charges. As used to be said among Southern Democrats, they'd vote for a yellow dog if their party nominated one. Campaigns therefore centered on rallying loyal troops and trying to woo the relatively small base of swing voters. As parties have declined, however, the proportion of swing voters has risen dramatically. Thus, a strategy of sharp personal attacks has more potential payoff in today's era of candidate-centered rather than partisan politics.

The degree to which such personal attacks drowned out discussion of major policy issues was also widely bemoaned during the 1988 campaign. For example, in October 1988 the *New York Times*/CBS News poll found that 46 percent of the electorate thought there had been less discussion of the issues than in the past, whereas just 8 percent thought there had been more. Michael Dukakis proclaimed at the outset that the election was not about ideology but about competence; George Bush then took up the challenge by directly impugning the governor's judgment. The Bush campaign ultimately succeeded in controlling the agenda, with the result that far more time was given to the issues of the pledge of allegiance, the Willie Horton furlough, and pollution in Boston Harbor than to how the candidates would govern the country.

Such a focus is symptomatic of an American politics that has become ever more personalized, in which the center of attention has turned from measures to men, from ideas to character. As Senator Bob Graham said to the Democratic Leadership Council in 1989,

The United States is going through the process of the McDonaldization of American politics. People are increasingly forming their partisan identifications by what they see on television. What they see on television is a national party dominated by its presidential candidates or that individual fortunate enough to be elected President. And when they look at our fast-food franchise and look at the Republicans' fast-food franchise on television they are selecting to buy their hamburgers at the other stand.[2]

If parties are considered as little more than fast-food franchises by their leaders, is it any wonder that the issues they discuss are generally lacking in beef?

For decades scholars have looked to the possibility of a critical realignment as the best hope for bringing major issues to the forefront and reaching decisive action on them.[3] Past realignments have been highly issue oriented, arousing electoral passions that have divided the electorate in a new and enduring way—and thereby redirected the course of American politics. Such critical political change is America's "surrogate for revolution," according to Walter Dean Burnham.[4] He and others have long maintained that without a realignment many key problems in American government will remain unresolved.

Throughout the 1980s there were ample signs that the long-awaited realignment and party revitalization might at last be under way. To some extent these expectations were realized; Republican identification in 1984 and 1988 grew to the point where the plurality of Democrats over Republicans reached its lowest level since 1952, when such measurements began. Yet such a realignment is hollow when the two parties involved continue to have a weak image in the public mind and an uncertain role in the future of American government. Realignment has thus been muted in the candidate-centered age in comparison to the electoral upheavals of the past.

In the first edition of this book, published just before the 1984 campaign, I wrote that conditions were beginning to look favorable for a party revitalization, but that

it remains to be seen whether partisan feelings can be rekindled in the midst of the hoopla of a presidential campaign when the candidates will undoubtedly receive the bulk of media attention. Even if the candidates act more as partisans than in the past, will a public accustomed to voting the man and not the party perceive the linkage between party and candidate? The answer will be of prime importance to the future of American political parties.[5]

Unfortunately, the answer is mostly a negative one. This chapter tells the fascinating story of how realignment occurred in the 1980s without much revitalization of partisanship in the electorate.

Indications of Party Revitalization after 1980

The events following the 1980 election provided as good an opportunity for party revitalization as had been seen in recent history. Regardless of how one evaluates the accomplishments of the Reagan presidency, one cannot deny the fact that it was able to initiate the most important reversal in the direction of American public policy in half a century. For once a candidate not only promised clear and dramatic changes but accomplished them as well. Reagan campaigned in 1980 on three major planks—cutting taxes, increasing military spending, and decreasing the rate of growth of federal spending on social services—each of which was accomplished within his first year of office. Most important, all of this was achieved with more unified party support than had been seen in Washington in decades. On the two key votes of 1981, for example—the tax cut and the budget resolution— Reagan held all but one Republican vote in the House. Unlike recent presidents, who have campaigned and governed largely on their own, staying relatively unencumbered by partisan ties or appeals, Reagan exercised a substantial role as party leader. And on the other side, the Democrats were forced into a far more unified stance than usual, much like Western settlers pulling their wagons into a circle to fend off attack. Wide differences over what the Democratic Party stands for persisted, but Reagan gave Democrats a clearer sense of what they were against. All told, party-line votes occurred on 50.6 percent of all House roll-call votes during the Reagan years—a figure unmatched since the final days of the New Deal (see Figure 5.1).

The 1984 and 1988 presidential campaigns offered further reasons to expect a revitalization of partisanship. In 1984 an incumbent president running for reelection was unchallenged for his party's nomination for the first time since 1956. Johnson was tested by Wallace in several primaries in 1964; Nixon was opposed by both left- and right-wing Republican hopefuls in 1972; Ford was barely able to turn back the Reagan challenge in 1976; and Carter was bitterly opposed by Kennedy in 1980. Not only was Reagan unchallenged, but his support of the party nearly matched the party's wholehearted support for him. For example, his campaign chairman, Edward J. Rollins, was quoted as saying, "No president in modern times has done more for his party than Reagan. He set up a political office in the White House to help congressional candidates. He cut hundreds of [television and radio] spots for them. He did fund-raisers."[6] Such behavior is strikingly different from that of other recent presidents. Perhaps the most extreme contrast is with Nixon, who in 1972 told Theodore White that it would be "stupid" for him to campaign for a "new Republican majority" rather than for a personal victory.[7]

On the Democratic side, for the first time since 1968 a true party insider and loyalist was nominated for the presidency in 1984. Unlike George McGovern and Jimmy Carter before him, Walter Mondale represented the traditional party mainstream. Whereas it is unlikely that party outsiders McGovern and Carter could have been nominated before the Democratic Party's rule changes, Mondale probably would have had an easier path to the nomination under the pre-reform system. As the near-consensus choice of the party regulars, Mondale was the first Democrat in years to run with the party rather than against it.

Not only did Mondale provide continuity with the traditional Democratic mainstream, but also, as Carter's vice president, he established a solid link to the most recent Democratic administration. In most elections voters are faced with a choice between an incumbent and an unfamiliar and untested alternative. Because of the continuity provided by Mondale, the choice in 1984 was more clearly between the performance and policies of the past two administrations. As Herbert Weisberg has put it, the 1984 campaign turned into a "double retrospective election," with both sides focusing on the recent past of the other.[8]

From a historical perspective, the Reagan–Mondale contest contained many elements similar to those of key elections in other realigning eras. The elections of 1896 and 1932 are usually thought to be the critical elections in the two most recent party realignments. Yet often overlooked in the study of these realignments is the importance of the elections following them— 1900 and 1936—which can be termed *cementing* elections, in that the change from the previous contest was solidified. In each case the party that had lost support during the critical election firmly opted for continuity in the next election rather than trying to shift away from what had been a disastrous course four years earlier. The Democrats reacted to William Jennings Bryan's 1896 landslide defeat by renominating him in 1900, thereby signaling to voters that the change in the Democratic coalition and platform was of a long-term nature. Similarly, in 1936 the Republicans chose Landon, who stood by the policies of Hoover rather than trying to dissociate himself from them. The point is that partisans may forgive a party that has gone astray once, but doing astray twice in a row may transform short-term change into long-term change. The Democrats' nomination of Carter's vice president in 1984 can thus be seen as an invitation for realignment history to repeat itself.

Another way in which realignment history seems to have been repeated is in the successor to the realigning president. Just as vice presidents Van Buren, T.

Roosevelt, and Truman carried on the legacy for realigning presidents Jackson, McKinley, and F. Roosevelt, respectively, so is Bush for Reagan. For the first time since Van Buren's 1836 victory, the incumbent vice president won a presidential election. If it can be said that Mondale helped keep Carter on voters' minds in 1984, then certainly Bush helped to keep Reagan in the forefront of attention in 1988. As Reagan himself said two days before the election, "I feel a little like I'm on the ballot myself this year."[9] The result was a further cementing of the realignment, or, as Seymour Martin Lipset has termed it, a "reaffirming election."[10]

Changing the Balance in Party Identification

From the inception of the National Election Studies in 1952 through 1980, Democrats consistently outnumbered Republicans by a ratio of approximately 1.7 to 1.0. As Table 9.1 shows, this ratio dropped dramatically in 1984, with Democrats outnumbering Republicans by less than 10 percent for the first time. The Democrats continued to decline in 1988, with Independents outnumbering them for the first time in a presidential election year. If one includes the Independent leaners with their respective partisan groups, the gap between the two parties is now just 6.2 percent. And, because Republicans turn out at higher rates, Democrats had only a 47.2-to-46.1 edge over the Republicans among those who said they voted in 1988. For the Republican Party this is the highest percentage ever, and for the Democratic Party the lowest.

Despite the sizable increase in Republican identifiers in 1984, their cohesiveness as a voting bloc was also

Table 9.1 Party identification, 1952–1988

	1952	1956	1960	1964	1968	1972	1976	1980	1984	1988
Democrats	47.2	43.6	45.3	51.7	45.4	40.4	39.7	40.8	37.0	35.2
Independents	22.6	23.4	22.8	22.8	29.1	34.7	36.1	34.5	34.2	35.7
Republicans	27.2	29.1	29.4	24.5	24.2	23.4	23.2	22.4	27.1	27.5
Apoliticals	3.1	3.8	2.5	0.9	1.4	1.4	0.9	2.2	1.7	1.6
Democratic plurality	20.0	14.5	15.9	27.2	21.2	17.0	16.5	18.4	9.9	7.7
Democrats plus Democratic leaners	56.8	49.9	51.6	61.0	55.2	51.5	51.5	52.3	47.8	47.0
Pure Independents	5.8	8.8	9.8	7.8	10.5	13.1	14.6	12.9	11.0	10.6
Republicans plus Republican leaners	34.3	37.4	36.1	30.2	32.9	33.9	32.9	32.6	39.5	40.8
Apoliticals	3.1	3.8	2.5	0.9	1.4	1.4	0.9	2.2	1.7	1.6
Democratic plurality	22.5	12.5	15.5	31.1	22.3	17.6	18.6	19.7	8.3	6.2

SOURCE: SRC/CPS National Election Studies.

close to an all-time high during Reagan's reelection campaign. Only 5 percent of all Republicans defected in 1984—well below their average presidential defection rate of 12 percent for 1952–1980. Furthermore, in 1988 Republican unity remained high; only 10 percent defected to Dukakis. Such cohesion is of no small consequence given that the candidate who has left his convention with the most united party has won every presidential election from 1964 to 1988. The Republicans typically start with two major advantages on this score. First, ever since the liberal Rockefeller wing was virtually banished from the party in 1964, they have been more ideologically cohesive than the Democrats. And second, the Republican nomination rules discourage long-drawn-out primary battles; candidates who lose in the early primaries are unable to pick up enough delegates to keep their campaign viable.[11]

Figure 9.1 illustrates the political importance of this rise in Republican identification and voting loyalty. As the minority party, the Republicans have in the past been heavily dependent on winning Democratic and Independent votes in order to win presidential elections. The relationship between the Republicans' dependence on their own identifiers and their electoral success was an almost perfect one from 1952 to 1980: the more they had to rely on Republican votes, the worse they did. For example, in their worst election year (1964) 76 percent of Republican votes came from Republican identifiers (including leaners), whereas in their best year (1972) the comparable figure was only 58 percent. Given this constant relationship, one would expect that since the Republican vote was so high in 1984, the percentage of it coming from Republi-

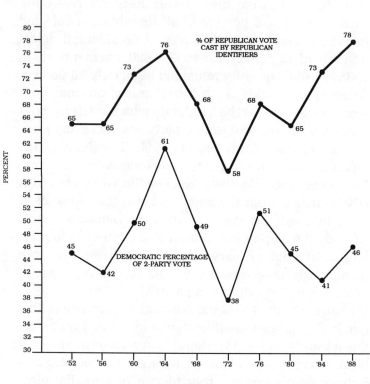

PERCENT

% OF REPUBLICAN VOTE
CAST BY REPUBLICAN
IDENTIFIERS

DEMOCRATIC PERCENTAGE
OF 2-PARTY VOTE

ELECTION YEAR

Figure 9.1   Democratic percentage of the vote as a function of the percentage of Republican votes cast by Republican identifiers

Source: SRC/CPS National Election Studies.

cans would be relatively low. However, the result of the growth of Republican identifiers and their voting loyalty is that the two lines in Figure 9.1 diverged from each other for the first time. The percentage of the 1984 Reagan vote that came from Republicans had been previously exceeded only in the Goldwater debacle of

1964. Yet Reagan's vote total was second only to Nixon's in 1972. Similarly, in 1988 Bush was able to win handily even though 78 percent of his votes came from Republicans—the highest ever for a GOP candidate.

The realignment has thus spurred a fundamental change in the Republicans' presidential strategy. No longer are they dependent on winning Democratic and Independent votes in presidential elections. With the new parity in size, both parties have come to focus more on simply holding on to their own base. This greater emphasis on appealing to one's own partisans is yet another reason to expect some strengthening of partisanship in the 1980s.

Such a strategy might not seem cohesive to the negative style of campaigning discussed at the beginning of this chapter. However, because partisanship is so much weaker now, much greater effort is required to reinforce it. Thus, although Bush may have needed to do little more than unify his party, such a task is far more difficult than it was several decades ago. The support of party identifiers can no longer be taken for granted, as was demonstrated by Bush's poor standing in the polls throughout the spring and summer of 1988. In this sense, Bush's negative campaigning was probably instrumental in convincing Republican voters to return home. Voters needed to be reminded of the stark differences between the nominees for the usual patterns to reassert themselves.

Perceptions of Party Differences

In the past, strong parties forced presidential candidates to moderate their views and move toward the center. This is no longer the case. In the mass media age candidates can appeal directly to the electorate rather than depending on the parties to get their message out. In order to attract media attention, though, differences must be accentuated. In addition, television's condensation of political rhetoric into "sound bites" has further contributed to the heightening of political differences. Because one can get only a McNugget on the air rather than a whole chicken (or even a wing or a leg), candidates have an incentive to go right for the jugular. The 1988 campaign was thus full of effective one-liners such as Bush's that Dukakis seemed to be against every weapon system since the slingshot. As Roger Ailes, Bush's media adviser said, "Every single thing I did from debates to rhetoric to speeches to media was designed to define the two of them and push them farther apart."[12]

It should therefore come as no surprise to find that the public's perception of major differences between the parties increased during the 1980s. When Reagan took over the Republican Party leadership, the percentage of the electorate seeing important differences in what the two major parties stand for jumped from the stable 46-to-52 percent range it occupied during the 1952–1976 period to between 58 and 63 percent from 1980–1988 (see Figure 9.2). This greater public perception of philosophical differences between the parties may well be one of the most long-lasting changes in American politics from the 1980s.

Yet this increase does not necessarily imply any revitalization of partisanship. The fact that citizens perceive differences between the parties does not make those differences relevant to them. The problem for the

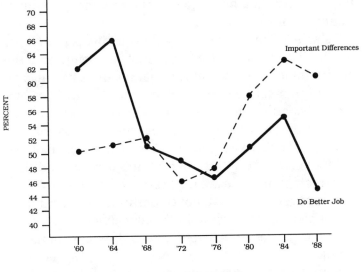

Figure 9.2 Perception of party differences and ability of parties to handle most important problem
Source: SRC/CPS National Election Studies.

parties, as noted in Chapter 4, has not been that fewer people see the policy differences between them. Rather, it has been the increasing failure to persuade them that one party will do a better job on whatever problem they consider to be most important.

As shown in Figure 9.2, in 1960 and 1964 substantially more people thought that parties mattered in terms of job performance than thought there were important differences between them. This is precisely a mirror image of what was found throughout the 1980s. In particular, in 1988 an all-time low of just 44.6 percent thought either the Democratic or the Republican

Party would do a better job on the problem they mentioned as most important.

Table 9.2 demonstrates that this decline is partly due
to the rise of new problems, such as drugs and the
environment, but that substantial declines can also be
found on ever-present problem categories. For example, people who mentioned foreign affairs, social
welfare, and business conditions (such as inflation and
unemployment) were 10 to 15 percent less likely in
1988 than in 1960 to think that one party would do a
better job.[13] As these are the bread-and-butter problems
that must be dealt with continually, such figures indicate a significant decline in the perceived relevance of
political parties for addressing standard governmental
problems.

Perhaps more worrisome, though, is the inability of
the parties to stake a claim to performing better on
problems that have assumed new importance in the
last decade—namely, the budget, drugs, and the environment. Balancing the budget has been a concern
throughout American history, but never so much as
during the massive deficit years of the 1980s. The Republicans were considered to be the party of fiscal constraint in 1960, and the relatively few people who were
most concerned with balancing the budget thought
they would handle it best. In contrast, roughly 30 percent named the budget as the most important problem
of 1988, but only 42 percent thought one party would
do a better job than the other. The divided government
of the 1980s allowed Republican leaders to blame
budget deficits on congressional spending for social
programs and Democratic leaders to put the blame on
the president's military buildup. With neither party

Table 9.2 Percentage seeing one party as doing a better job on most important problem, by issue category, 1960 and 1988

Issue	1960	1988
Social welfare	64.7	50.5
	(255)	(364)
Foreign affairs	63.2	49.0
	(940)	(102)
Economics and business	62.3	51.3
	(114)	(156)
National defense	65.8	61.4
	(117)	(57)
Agriculture	67.3	27.3
	(104)	(11)
Union-management relations	48.6	—
	(37)	
Balanced budget	76.0	42.4
	(25)	(495)
Public order	—	50.9
		(57)
Racial	38.8	42.9
	(103)	(14)
Moral decay	—	38.0
		(50)
Abortion, women's rights	—	77.3
		(22)
Environment	—	31.7
		(82)
Drugs	—	31.0
		(213)

NOTE: Number of cases in parentheses.
SOURCE: SRC/CPS National Election Studies.

really in charge, and each pointing the finger at the other, is it any wonder that the majority could not judge which would do a better job?

Similarly, how can people assess which party would do better on a new problem such as drugs when the government's response is not to implement a party's promises but rather to appoint a "drug czar" to oversee the situation? Like the energy crisis of the 1970s, the problem has been farmed out from the normal channels of government to an individual who has supposedly been given extraordinary powers. When problems are dealt with by individuals, voters tend to view them through a personalized framework. They can judge whether they think individuals have been or will be effective, but the link to a political party is weak. For example, of those who mentioned drugs as the most important problem facing the government in 1988, 70 percent thought that either Bush or Dukakis would do a better job, whereas only 31 percent could judge which of the parties would do better.[14]

The personalization of almost every issue also explains the decreased perception of party relevance to continuing problems such as the economy. As noted in Chapter 8, the fact that the economic program of the 1980s was popularly known as "Reaganomics" rather than "Republican economics" says much about how the public viewed it. Indeed, when people were asked why they thought the nation's economy had either improved or worsened in 1984, 21.1 percent explicitly said the president was responsible, compared with only 0.5 percent who named one of the two parties.

In sum, the crucial problem for the political parties is not to convince the public that there are important philosophical differences between them. More than ever in recent history, people see these differences. Rather, the parties need to reestablish their importance in relation to the crucial issues of the day. In order to regain the level of prominence they formerly held in the public mind, the parties need people to make the connection between them and what is done by government to address the most important problems of the time.

More on the Role of the Media

As a result of changes in political communications over the last few decades this task has become increasingly difficult. The media are anxious to cover stories about the differences between the parties—especially if they can be dramatized with pithy sound bites from party leaders. However, presenting the case for one or the other party's handling of a major problem involves offering a value judgment. And the media increasingly shy away from either value judgments or endorsements.

Television reporting has of course been constrained from the outset by the Fairness Doctrine. American newspapers, on the other hand, originated as largely partisan enterprises. As Lance Bennett writes, "Reporting involved the political interpretation of events. People bought a newspaper knowing what its political perspective was, and knowing that political events would be filtered through that perspective."[15] Such partisan reporting has been gradually displaced throughout this century by objective reporting. The economic success of papers such as the *New York Times* in presenting the news in a nonbiased fashion led many others to adopt this technique. Furthermore, influential journalists such as Walter Lippmann argued that it was a reporter's responsibility to report the facts without interjecting his or her own viewpoint. Thus, although objective reporting started as a technique to sell newspapers, it eventually developed into a value, as Lou Cannon observes.[16]

Political commentary or endorsements are now strictly confined to the editorial pages in virtually all U.S. newspapers. Yet even on the editorial pages newspapers are much less likely to take a stand than in the past. Since 1932 *Editor and Publisher* magazine has surveyed the country's newspapers in the fall of presidential election years to determine how many papers have endorsed each candidate. In the 1930s only about 5 percent of all newspapers declined to make an endorsement for president, as shown in Figure 9.3. This proportion gradually increased in the 1940s and 1950s, leveling off at close to 25 percent in the 1960s and 1970s. The 1980s display the biggest increase in newspaper neutrality in the survey's long history. In 1980 and 1984 roughly 35 percent of newspapers chose not to offer a presidential endorsement, and in 1988 more than half (55 percent) took this route.

The great jump in newspaper neutrality in 1988 no doubt stems partially from dissatisfaction with the candidates, as evidenced in the quotation from the *Washington Post* at the beginning of this chapter. Yet there are solid economic reasons for the acceleration of the trend in the 1980s, which should continue to discourage many newspapers from making endorsements in the future. As the resources necessary to keep a news-

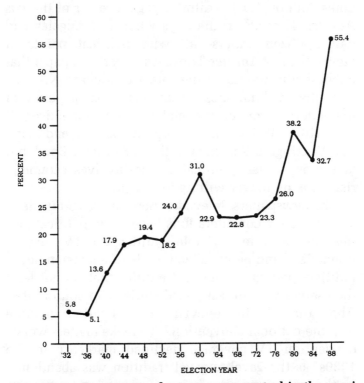

Figure 9.3   Percentage of newspapers neutral in the presidential race, 1932–1988

Source: *Editor and Publisher* surveys, 1932–1988, as reported in Milton C. Cummings, Jr., and David Wise, *Democracy under Pressure* (New York: Harcourt Brace Jovanovich, 1989), p. 331.

paper afloat have escalated in recent years, many have been forced out of business. The result has been that a single paper now typically controls its local market, even in some of the larger metropolitan areas. "The disappearance of competing papers means that those that endorse are no longer one voice among many," notes Anthony Day, editorial page director of the *Los Angeles Times*.[17] In the days when Los Angeles had half a dozen papers—all with political points of view—the *Los Angeles Times* was a partisan paper that unabashedly promoted the career of Richard Nixon.[18] Now that it dominates the market it has a policy of nonendorsement for national or statewide offices. It was willing to irk Miami Dolphins fans by endorsing the Washington Redskins in the 1983 Super Bowl, but taking a partisan political stance involves economic risks it is no longer willing to accept.

Like newspapers, television news is also a business, and economic considerations have made political parties less and less visible entities on TV. In the dramatized and personalized world of television news, political parties are abstract entities that do not lend themselves well to fast-paced stories and sound bites. About the only time television covers parties anymore is at the national conventions. To make matters worse, convention TV coverage declined markedly in the 1980s, as the gavel-to-gavel tradition was abandoned by the major networks.

It is interesting to note that financial considerations led television to adopt the gavel-to-gavel standard in the first place. Reuven Frank, who played a key role in developing TV convention coverage in the 1950s, writes that it saved money to broadcast extra hours from the convention hall and "to shut down the studios in New York, sending home, unpaid, the expensive union electricians, stagehands, musicians and actors."[19] Because many TV reporters made their reputations at the conventions, gavel-to-gavel coverage was continued as a loss-leader for the network news divi-

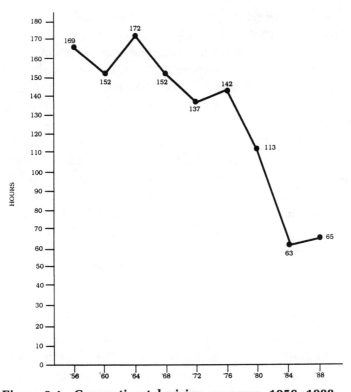

Figure 9.4   Convention television exposure, 1956–1988
Source: Calculated from data reported in Byron E. Shafer, *Bifurcated Politics: Evolution and Reform in the National Party Convention* (Cambridge, Mass.: Harvard University Press, 1988), p. 274; updated for 1988.

sions long after the death of live TV. As late as 1976, CBS and NBC covered the conventions for longer than they were actually in session.[20] But as can be seen in Figure 9.4, television coverage of conventions declined dramatically in the 1980s. The three major networks combined devoted about 160 hours each election year to the pre-reform conventions of 1956–1968; however, in both 1984 and 1988 they allocated only about 40 percent of this amount.

Considering how little real news now occurs at party conventions, one can hardly fault the networks for their lack of coverage. Since the rise of presidential primaries, conventions have become tightly scripted affairs with a predictable outcome. Both parties have learned that there are real dangers associated with having exciting internal debates broadcast on live television. The networks will devote additional coverage if there is a showdown at the convention, and viewers will be more likely to tune in to watch the fireworks. What is good for drawing television attention, however, often works against uniting the party and attracting Independent and swing voters. Thus, there is little incentive for the parties to welcome any activity at future conventions that cannot be carefully scripted.

To use Walter Bagehot's terms, the national nominating convention has undergone a transformation from an efficient to a dignified institution. The convention is no longer where the nomination is made, any more than the British monarchy is where government decisions are made in Britain. Both are long-standing institutions, and each plays a role in legitimating choices, but they have been superseded by more modern institutions that make the actual political decisions. While this sort of dignified status might be most fitting for the British monarchy, as Bagehot pointed over a century ago, it does not suit the American party convention very well. The convention is the one chance every four years for the parties to demonstrate publicly the crucial role they play in the governmental process.[21] As with the rise of newspaper neutrality,

TV's reduced coverage of the only full-fledged party gatherings has had the effect of making the public more likely to look upon the parties with indifference.

Continued Partisan Neutrality

Perhaps the most important table in the first edition of this book was Table 4.4, which demonstrated that the public had become increasingly neutral toward the two major parties between 1952 and 1980. This information is reproduced and updated through 1988 in Table 9.3. The top section shows that the steady growth in the neutral-neutral category was only slightly reversed in 1984 and 1988. Over 30 percent of the population remains neutral toward both parties despite the outward signs of party revitalization.

Given the indications of party realignment in 1984 and 1988, these data take on increased importance, and it is useful to present them separately by party as well. The major finding is that although the Republican image has become notably more positive since 1976, each party is still seen neutrally by over 40 percent of the population—that is, the electorate sees both Democrats and Republicans less positively as well as negatively than in 1952. Each party should of course be concerned about inducing the public to view it more favorably, but their joint concern should be to motivate the public to think more about them.

In sum, all the positive signs of party revitalization in the 1980s have done little to reverse the decline of partisanship in the electorate. An average of 30 percent of the population had nothing to say about either party in 1984 and 1988, in spite of the realignment. It is of

Table 9.3 Attitudes toward the parties, 1952–1988

| | Both parties combined | | | | | |
	Negative- negative	Negative- neutral	Neutral- neutral	Positive- negative	Positive- neutral	Positive- positive
1952	3.6	9.7	13.0	50.1	18.1	5.5
1956	2.9	9.0	15.9	40.0	23.3	8.9
1960	1.9	7.5	16.8	41.4	24.2	8.3
1964	4.4	11.2	20.2	38.4	20.6	5.0
1968	10.0	13.8	17.3	37.5	17.4	4.1
1972	7.9	12.6	29.9	30.3	14.7	4.7
1976	7.5	11.8	31.3	31.1	13.7	4.5
1980	5.0	8.6	36.5	27.3	17.7	4.8
1984	3.0	7.7	35.8	30.3	18.0	4.1
1988	3.5	7.8	30.3	34.0	17.8	6.5

| | Republican Party | | |
	Negative	Neutral	Positive
1952	35.0	28.2	36.8
1958	30.5	34.2	35.3
1960	29.6	35.5	34.9
1964	35.4	40.9	23.7
1968	32.6	37.1	30.3
1972	31.8	44.6	23.6
1976	34.8	45.9	19.3
1980	24.8	52.1	23.1
1984	26.1	48.7	25.2
1988	26.4	44.2	29.4

| | Democratic Party | | |
	Negative	Neutral	Positive
1952	32.3	25.3	42.4
1956	24.2	30.0	45.8
1960	22.2	31.5	46.3
1964	23.0	31.4	45.6
1968	38.6	28.6	32.8
1972	26.9	42.4	30.7
1976	23.3	42.2	34.5
1980	21.1	47.3	31.6
1984	18.8	48.8	32.4
1988	22.5	42.1	35.4

SOURCE: SRC/CPS National Election Studies.

some interest that many of these people nevertheless considered themselves Republicans or Democrats, or felt closer to one party or the other.[22] But given such respondents' lack of cognitive associations with the parties, I would question whether their supposed party identifications have much meaning.

On the other hand, some analysts have questioned the neutrality measure because of concerns about whether many people can express their images of the parties. As Stephen Craig writes, "Given the limited extent to which most Americans are capable of articulating a 'rational' explanation for their feelings toward either of the major parties, we have serious reservations about the validity of this approach."[23] The major weakness of Craig's critique is that there is no reason to believe that the articulation problem is any greater in the 1980s than it was in the 1950s. If articulation were really the reason for voters' increasing failure to say anything (either positive or negative) about the parties, then the same pattern should hold for similarly worded open-ended questions. For example, what people say they like and dislike about the presidential candidates should also be found to be increasingly lacking in content. This is not the case, however. Whereas the percentage of the population with nothing to say about the parties rose from 10 percent in 1952 to a high point of 34 percent in 1980, the percentage saying nothing about the candidates remained in the narrow range of 4 to 10 percent during the same period. Therefore, it is clear that people have not become less articulate in response to open-ended questions in general. As John Geer concludes, "when an open-ended question addresses a highly salient subject, people respond."[24] The problem is that parties are no longer such subjects.

Political Polarization in the Candidate-Centered Age

Because parties are viewed with greater indifference now, people's claims that they are Democrats or Republicans often mean something quite different from what they did several decades ago. Although party labels remain intact and enduring for many voters, all too often they lack the depth and meaning formerly associated with them. The traditional concept of party identification held that people had images of the parties based on their past experience and that these images led to a standing decision to support a party's candidates. As new candidates came along, partisanship acted as a perceptual screen, influencing how people evaluated them. Parties thus were the key factors that polarized people into rival political camps.

With the decline of political parties, a vacuum was created in the structuring of electoral attitudes, thereby setting voters adrift. Like nature, politics abhors a vacuum, and presidential candidates were the most logical force to take the place of parties in this respect. Candidates rather than parties have therefore become the central objects of political polarization. The gradual shift in the focus of American politics from parties to candidates is an important historical trend spanning the last several decades, as earlier chapters of this book have demonstrated. In particular, the cementing election of 1984 and the polarizing candidacy of Ronald Reagan stimulated the trend toward candidate-centered politics to new heights.

Indeed, Democrats and Republicans in the 1980s differed far more in their evaluations of the presidential candidates than in their attitudes toward the political parties themselves. This can best be illustrated by a comparison of the mean ratings that Democratic and Republican identifiers and leaners had of the candidates and parties on the like/dislike measures. Table 9.4 compares data from 1952 to the high point thus far of candidate-centered polarization in 1984. It demonstrates that in 1952 the two rival partisan camps were divided more by their evaluations of the parties than by their evaluation of the candidates, whereas the situation had been dramatically reversed by 1984. Overall, candidate polarization increased from 3.7 to 5.7 comments per respondent, while polarization on party images declined from an average of 4.9 to 3.5 remarks.

Figure 9.5 portrays the historical progression of these two opposing trends in political polarization. It demonstrates that party polarization declined rather steadily from 1952 to 1972 but has risen somewhat since then. From 1952 to 1968 this decline was counterbalanced by an increase in the degree to which Democrats and Republicans were divided by their assessments of the candidates. During this period the total level of political polarization remained virtually unchanged, as the percentage accounted for by candidate evaluations increased gradually from 42.7 to 56.3 percent. In the elections from 1972 to 1980, the focus on candidates continued, while the total level of polarization declined sharply; neither candidate nor party images sharply divided Democratic and Republican identifiers. More than ever before, candidate coalitions crossed the increasingly tenuous boundaries between the parties.

Such boundaries were reinvigorated during the

Table 9.4 Polarization between Democratic and Republican identifiers/leaners, 1952 and 1984 (mean ratings)

	Democratic identifiers/ leaners	Republican identifiers/ leaners	polarization
Candidates			
1984			
Mondale	1.19	−1.39	2.58
Reagan	−1.47	1.65	3.12
			5.70
1952			
Stevenson	1.14	−.53	1.67
Eisenhower	.19	2.18	1.99
			3.66
Parties			
1984			
Democratic Party	1.07	−.62	1.69
Republican Party	−.81	.98	1.79
			3.48
1952			
Democratic Party	1.08	−1.33	2.41
Republican Party	−.84	1.67	2.51
			4.92

Total polarization: 1952 = 8.58   1984 = 9.18
Candidate-centered polarization: 1952 = 42.7%
    1984 = 62.1%

SOURCE: SRC/CPS National Election Studies.
NOTE: Candidate-centered polarization = candidate polarization/total polarization.

realignment of 1984–1988. As demonstrated in Figure 9.1, Republican victories were no longer dependent on gaining defections from Democrats. Yet the increased polarization between Democrats and Republicans can be traced far more to candidate than to party images. In

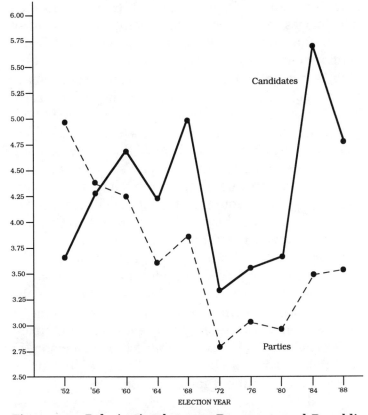

Figure 9.5   Polarization between Democrats and Republicans on candidate and party images
Source: SRC/CPS National Election Studies.

both 1984 and 1988 the ratio between candidate versus party polarization exceeded that recorded in any previous presidential election for which we have survey data.

Ronald Reagan will probably go down in history as the most polarizing candidate in the second half of the twentieth century,[25] but little of this was translated into images of his party. For example, 43 percent of those who reported voting for Reagan in 1984 had a neutral view of the Republican Party, whereas in 1952 only 24 percent of Eisenhower voters had such a tenuous image of the party. In contrast, when great historical figures such as Lincoln, Bryan, or F. Roosevelt polarized the electorate, opinions concerning them were quickly incorporated into the party images, thereby polarizing voters along partisan lines as well.

In sum, responsible-party-government advocates got the clear polarization and ideological differences between the parties they had long sought during the 1980s. However, it did not occur in the kind of partisan-dominated environment they had envisioned. The responsible-party model can hardly work in an atmosphere in which individual candidates dominate the political scene, with political parties struggling to maintain a modest degree of relevance amidst rampant split-ticket voting. The continuing phenomenon of split-ticket voting provides the last piece of the puzzle of realignment without revitalization.

Split-Ticket Voting during the Realignment

In an electorate less motivated by partisanship, realignment is easier to induce as well as less meaningful. If one were to apply the theories of *The American Voter* to the survey data of the 1980s, one would expect to find the change in partisanship to have an effect on party control at all levels of government. Such has not been the case. Voting the man, not the party, has now become part of the American consensus or creed. For example, a 1986 survey by Larry Sabato found that 92 percent agreed with the statement "I always vote for the person who I think is best, regardless of what party they belong to." On the flip side of the coin, only 14 percent in the same survey agreed with the statement "I always support the candidates of just one party."[26] Such public unanimity is a great rarity in American politics.

Because candidates are increasingly judged on their own character and experience rather than on the party they represent and its ideas, coattails have withered away, and divided government has become the rule. By the end of Bush's first term, the same party will have controlled the presidency and the House for just fourteen of the last forty years. When Eisenhower was reelected in 1956 with a Democratic Congress, it marked the first time in a century that a presidential election had resulted in split control of the two branches; by the 1980s, such an outcome had become commonplace. In 44 percent of all congressional districts in 1984, the party that won the presidential race lost in the congressional contest. This percentage matches the historical high for this measure, set in 1972 when Nixon won by the largest margin ever but the Republicans gained only twelve additional House seats (see Figure 1.1). In 1988 the proportion of congressional districts with split outcomes declined to 34 percent, but the Republicans actually lost seats in both the House and Senate despite Bush's forty-state sweep. Furthermore, on the state level, the 1988 election left a twentieth-century low of only eighteen states with unified party control of both legislative houses and the governorship.

Such aggregate figures, though instructive as broad indicators of systemic patterns, can sometimes be misleading as measures of behavior on the individual level. From Table 9.5 it can be seen that although partisan behavior did not decline in 1984 and 1988, it was not revitalized across the board either. Certainly party identification was a more meaningful predictor of the presidential vote. If one includes Independent leaners as partisans, then the percentage casting party-line votes for president reached new highs in 1984 and 1988. As would be expected from the aggregate figures, however, this greater partisan behavior did *not* extend to the congressional level. Whereas the pattern once was for more party-line voting in lower-level elections, just the opposite is now the case. In the case of both House and Senate elections, party-line voting remains well below the comparable figures from the 1952–1964 period.

Similarly, in 1984 and 1988 split-ticket voting remained quite high by historical standards, though down somewhat from the high point in 1980. One should not make too much of the decrease in ticket splitting between president and House: the 1980 figure is inflated by the Anderson vote. Also, the record high for ticket splitting between Senate and House voting in 1980 now appears to be a blip in the time series because of the abnormal number of strong Senate challengers that year. With these factors properly taken into account, it thus seems that split-ticket voting remains at alarmingly high levels for the future of party government.

The upshot, as David Broder writes, is that "when voters won't make the hard choice of which party should govern, the only government you can get is gov-

Table 9.5 Trends in split-ticket and party-line voting, 1952–1988

	1952	1956	1960	1964	1968	1972	1976	1980	1984	1988
Split-ticket voting										
President-House	12	16	14	15	26	30	25	34	25	25
Senate-House	9	10	9	18	22	23	23	31	20	27
Local	27	30	27	41	48	56	NA	59	52	NA
Party-line voting (excluding leaners)[a]										
House	67	70	69	69	60	58	57	53	54	56
Senate	65	68	69	67	62	56	53	55	55	55
President	63	63	67	67	56	50	55	54	59	61
Party-line voting (including leaners)[b]										
House	80	82	80	79	74	75	72	69	70	74
Senate	79	80	79	79	73	69	69	71	72	72
President	77	76	79	79	69	67	74	68	80	82

SOURCE: SRC/CPS National Election Studies.
a. Democratic or Republican identifiers vote for a candidate of their party for the office listed.
b. Democrat or Independent Democrats vote for a Democratic candidate, and Republican or Independent Republicans vote for a Republican candidate.

ernment by improvisation."[27] Yet, at the same time, the strong rhetoric of the candidate-centered campaign leaves politicians with little flexibility (such as "Read my lips, no new taxes!"). The inevitable result of either openness to compromise or the authority to carry out a program is the continuing paralysis of American government.

Given the continuing weakness of the public image of both parties, one must question whether the change in party identification in favor of the Republicans has much substantive meaning. One possible explanation for this shift is that partisanship has now become so weak that people are shifting it with their presidential vote. If party identification has become nothing more than an indicator of short-term presidential preference, this would explain why party-line voting so increased on the presidential, but not the congressional, level. Although this is a plausible hypothesis, it seems unlikely given that the same circumstances of weak partisanship and a Republican landslide occurred in both 1972 and 1980 without affecting the distribution of party identification at all.

What made the 1984 election different, in my view, was the clear contrast between the performance of the incumbent Republican administration and the Democratic administration it replaced. For once the choice was not between the present and an uncertain alternative future. Rather, the Reagan–Mondale contest was one between the recent past and a present that had seen major changes. Such a choice was conducive not only to vote switching but to partisan switching as well. Until the Democrats regain control of the presidency and prove that they can do something different, it is doubtful that these shifts will be substantially reversed. Indeed, with continuing peace and prosperity in 1988, this new pattern was reconfirmed.

However, even assuming that the Republican surge is a long-lasting one, it will be of limited importance as long as partisan attitudes remain so weak and split-ticket voting so prevalent. Given the most ideal conditions for party revitalization in decades, these indicators showed little change in 1984 and 1988. Parties may be stronger than ever before organizationally[28] and more unified at the elite level, but that has not made the public pay more attention to them. As Joseph Schlesinger has argued, the very weakness of partisanship in the electorate has stimulated the recent growth of regularized party organization.[29] In this sense, the revitalization of some aspects of American political parties has been an adaptation to an electoral process increasingly oriented around candidates. The candidate-centered age will apparently be with us for a long time to come, regardless of whether the next political era is a Democratic or Republican one.

10

The 1992 Election: Ross Perot and the Independent Voter

More than any other election in recent memory, the 1992 presidential campaign demonstrated the weak hold of the two major political parties on the American public. As previous chapters of this book have discussed, party decline in the electorate is hardly a new phenomenon. What was unique about the 1992 election was the manifestation of party decline in the historically unparalleled independent presidential candidacy of Ross Perot.

It would be stretching the reader's imagination to argue that earlier versions of this book foretold anything like the emergence of Ross Perot on the national scene. After all, who could have predicted that a billionaire businessman would suddenly decide to spend millions of his own money to finance an independent run for the White House? Although Perot's actions may have been unpredictable, the circumstances he took advantage of have been evident in American politics for a long time.

Most important among the developments that made Ross Perot's meteoric rise possible is the decline of

American political parties. A key premise of the Perot campaign was that political parties are basically irrelevant as long as a candidate can get enough time on TV to be heard by the American public. Perot got his start from TV talk shows that enabled him to take his case directly to the American public. Largely eschewing personal appearances and rallies in the last month of the campaign, Perot relied primarily on televised debates and thirty-minute infomercials to present his ideas.

Political leaders have been appealing directly to the American public for quite some time, with the consequence that issues have become increasingly seen in terms of candidates rather than parties. Thus Ross Perot followed the same course as other recent presidential candidates. He just skipped the customary step of nominally identifying himself as either a Democrat or a Republican to gain an initial political foothold.

Perot's message that things were a mess in Washington also had a very familiar ring to it. Unlike presidential candidates who used this line in the past, such as Dwight Eisenhower, Jimmy Carter, or Ronald Reagan, Perot did not blame one of the parties but rather the inefficiency of party politics. The term "gridlock" became one of his favorite watchwords, evoking the inability of either party to get things done. As a successful businessman, Perot argued that the government should be run more like a business. Lines of authority are clear in a business, as they had not been in American government for most of the post-1968 period. In particular, the coexistence of a Republican president and a Democratic Congress during the Reagan-Bush years led to the politics of the "blame game," with each side pointing the finger at the other for the inability to address the nation's problems.

Interestingly, Perot's proposed solution to partisan gridlock was not to clarify the lines of authority by placing the presidency and Congress in the same hands. Rather, he argued that voters should ignore partisanship and place someone without ties to either party at the top. In the end, 19 percent of the electorate cast their votes for his nonpartisan candidacy. This marked the highest percentage an independent presidential candidate had won in the eighty years since Theodore Roosevelt bolted from the Republicans to run his Bull Moose campaign. Perot would likely have done even better on election day had he not inexplicably dropped out of the presidential race in the summer. During May and June of 1992, Perot actually led both Bush and Clinton in a number of national and key state polls. His sudden departure from the race in July alienated many who might have voted for him in November.[1]

Ironically, just when support for Perot peaked, in June, the University of California Press released a book on voting behavior, *The Myth of the Independent Voter.* Bruce Keith and his coauthors challenge the notion that voters are less tied to political parties than they used to be. Their conclusion states that "the surface-level increase in Independents does not portend a decline in political stability, the decay of the political system, nor any of the other unwelcome developments heralded by some scholars. In fact, we might go so far as to say that it portends very little at all."[2] Endorsing this view, Norman Ornstein writes that *The Myth of the Independent Voter* "systematically demolishes" the conventional wisdom of "a large and growing army of independent voters threatening the stability of the two-party system." Similarly, Anthony King states, "If the authors are right (and they almost certainly are), an embarrassingly large proportion of the received wisdom of the 1970s and 1980s is going to have to be junked."[3]

Although Ross Perot's 1992 campaign decimated a fair amount of conventional political wisdom, the thesis that parties are in decline emerged looking even sounder. Indeed, if ever there was evidence of the independence from partisanship of many American voters, the Perot phenomenon confirms it. The preceding chapter on the elections of 1984 and 1988 concluded that realignment in favor of the Republicans would be hollow as long as partisanship in the electorate remained so weak. The 1992 election results clearly support such a conclusion, and the survey results reviewed in this chapter show how the lack of support for either party opened the way for Ross Perot.

The Continuing Evidence for Dealignment

Two days before election day in 1992, the *Los Angeles Times* published an interview with the noted British psephologist David Butler. When asked what had struck him about this election, Butler responded: "Two words that aren't used in the election. One is 'Democrat' and the other is 'Republican.' You see billboards, and they're selling the candidate, but people are not tying themselves much up with the Bush label, let alone the Republican label. This is one of the areas of total difference between Britain and the United States. In Britain, we think in terms of party ... We aren't voting for Kinnock or Major, we are voting for a Conservative or Labour government."[4]

One scarcely needs to be from another country to be struck by this pattern in American politics. With less than two weeks to go in the 1992 campaign, I spent several days in Santa Barbara, California, where a hotly contested House race was underway. Businessman Michael Huffington spent millions of dollars (mostly from his personal fortune) seeking election from California's Twenty-second Congressional District. His main opponent, Gloria Ochoa—a local elected official—was also well funded, to the tune of about $650,000. As one might imagine from the amount of money being spent on this campaign, there were many billboards and yard signs around town for both candidates. And because the Santa Barbara TV market matched that of the congressional district pretty well, both candidates invested heavily in TV commercials. After several days in Santa Barbara, I felt I had learned a fair amount about these two candidates. Yet what I most wanted to know about each candidate was something that could not be ascertained from the candidates' advertising. Neither Huffington nor Ochoa said which party they represented, nor could I even infer their party affiliations from the sorts of appeals they made.[5]

Such was not always the case in American politics. During the 1992 campaign David Broder made this point in a column comparing Bill Clinton to John F.

Kennedy, noting that "while Clinton has distanced himself from the Democratic Congress, Kennedy sounded a call for a party victory, not just a change of tenants in the White House."[6] Both Kennedy and Clinton came into office with strong Democratic majorities in both houses of Congress, but in Clinton's case this was more of a coincidence than the result of strongly partisan behavior by either the politicians or the voters.

The dealignment of the electorate from political parties since Kennedy's era can be demonstrated by a variety of indicators, as shown in Table 10.1. Of these, the variable most closely watched in the academic literature over the last four decades has been the percentage identifying with a political party. In 1992 this figure reached an all-time low for presidential election years of just 61 percent.[7] Hedrick Smith, in his 1988 best-seller *The Power Game,* writes that "The most important phenomenon of American politics in the past quarter century has been the rise of independent voters who have at times outnumbered Republicans."[8] The 1992 data show that nonpartisans now outnumber Democrats as well. The numbers are: 38 percent Independent, 36 percent Democrat, 25 percent Republican, and 1 percent apolitical. And as has always been the case, young citizens remain significantly less likely to adopt a party label. Only half of the election study respondents under 30 years of age considered themselves either Democrats or Republicans in 1992.

The authors of *The Myth of the Independent Voter* dismiss such statistics as misleading. They note that when asked "Do you think of yourself as closer to the

Table 10.1 Key indicators of dealignment, 1952-1992 (in percentages)

Year	Identifies with a party	Splits ticket between President and House	Splits ticket between Senate and House	Neutral toward both parties	Positive toward one party and negative toward the other	One party does a better job on most important problem
1952	75	12	9	13	50	—
1956	73	16	10	16	40	—
1960	75	14	9	17	41	62
1964	77	15	18	20	38	66
1968	70	26	22	17	38	52
1972	64	30	23	30	30	49
1976	63	25	23	31	31	46
1980	64	34	31	37	27	50
1984	64	25	20	36	31	55
1988	63	25	27	30	34	45
1992	61	36	25	32	34	51

SOURCE: SRC/CPS National Election Studies.

Republican Party or to the Democratic Party?" about two-thirds of those without a partisan affiliation will say they lean one way or the other. Furthermore, they show that such partisan leanings are strongly related to the vote. Averaging the figures from 1952 to 1992, one finds that Independents who leaned toward the GOP voted for the Republican presidential candidate 84 percent of the time and that Independents who leaned toward the Democrats voted 69 percent Democratic. These voting patterns lead the authors to argue that Independents "are largely closet Democrats and Republicans."[9]

A different view is offered by Larry Sabato, who writes that "the reluctance of 'leaners' to admit their real party identification in itself is worrisome because it reveals a sea change in attitudes about political parties and their proper role in our society."[10] If increased independence does indicate a movement of partisans into the closet, the question arises what is now so attractive about the closet. The best available data on this question can be found in the 1980 National Election Study. Respondents who called themselves Independents or replied "no preference" to the initial party identification question were handed a list of eleven statements and asked to say which ones described their reasons for identifying themselves as such. The percentage that checked each statement is displayed below.

75% I decide on the person not the party.
59% I decide on the issue not the party label.
36% The parties almost never deliver on their promises.

30%   I support both Democrats and Republicans.
20%   I'm not much interested in politics.
17%   I don't know enough to make a choice.
15%   Neither party stands for what I think is important.
14%   I like both parties about the same.
13%   I'm Independent because of the way I feel about what Jimmy Carter has been doing.
 5%   My parents were Independent and I am too.
 4%   I dislike both parties.

The primary reasons for nonpartisanship are therefore normative values, the belief that one should decide on the person and the issues rather than strictly on the party.

At the outset of *The Myth of the Independent Voter,* the authors retell the old story of the voter who remarks, "Me, I vote the man, not party. Hoover, Landon, Dewey, Eisenhower ... " and go on to assert that "most Americans resemble that man."[11] Yet never in their analysis do they examine data regarding whether people report voting consistently for the same party as much as in the past. Such a time series exists and is inconsistent with their story. As shown in Figure 1.2, the percentage of voters who reported voting for different parties for president increased from 29 percent in 1952 to 57 percent in 1980. Unfortunately, this survey question has not been repeated since 1980. Given the recent volatility of the Republican presidential vote, from 59 percent in 1984 to 38 percent in 1992, it is hardly likely that one would find an increase in the proportion of voters who claim to have always supported the same party.

The crux of Keith et al.'s data presentation is simply that there has been little change over time in the proportion of the presidential vote explained by the party identification measure. Similarly, a recent article by Warren Miller concluded, "There is no indication from any recent election that party identification is less relevant to the vote decision in the 1980s than it was three decades earlier."[12] A crucial weakness of both works, however, is their focus on a single voting decision. Unlike voters in parliamentary systems, Americans cast a number of votes all at the same time. To ignore the pattern of these votes is to examine only a small slice of political behavior. Examining a wider spectrum of voting choices reveals a clear decline over time in the relevance of partisanship.

If party affiliation is just as meaningful as it used to be, one should find a consistently high level of straight-ticket voting over time. This is not the case. Table 10.1 shows that the percentage of voters splitting their ticket for President and Representative reached an all-time high of 36 percent in 1992. Of course, much of the increase in 1992 can be traced to the high level of support for Ross Perot—as any vote for Perot is by definition a split-ticket vote. Among Bush and Clinton voters, only 22 percent crossed over to the other party in voting for the House of Representatives. Yet without Perot in the race, ticket-splitting would probably have been somewhat higher than this because Perot voters appear to be particularly likely to split their votes between the two major parties.[13] All told, if Perot had not been on the ballot, ticket-splitting between President and House probably would have been about 25 percent, which also happens to be the percentage voting for different parties for the House and Senate in 1992.

One might look at this 25 percent figure optimistically by noting that in each two-party pairing three-quarters of all voters continued to vote for candidates of the same party. However, if people voted completely at random for two offices with two candidates each, half of their votes would still appear to be party votes simply by chance. Given more opportunities to split their ticket, it is likely that more people would do so, as the Perot campaign demonstrated. Voting patterns for those who cast presidential, House, and Senate ballots in 1992 show that only 57 percent cast a straight ticket for all three offices. Furthermore, while the two-party system usually limits the number of choices for each office, the complex American system of government presents the electorate with a wide array of offices to vote on. One recent study looked at voting behavior for five statewide offices in Ohio and found that the majority of voters split their tickets.[14]

This book's research design employs a number of measures to understand various aspects of the public's attitudes toward the parties. Of all the indicators of party decline covered here, the open-ended measurement of neutrality toward the parties is the most striking. The third segment of Table 10.1 shows that the percentage of respondents neutral toward both parties on the like/dislike questions remained above 30 percent in 1992. Compared to the decline of party identification, the rise of neutrality in party images has occurred over a longer period of time and has been a far more pronounced trend. The major reason for this discrepancy is that party identification involves a process of self-labeling and is therefore more likely to be stable than other political attitudes.[15] This stability can be seen as a theoretical weakness of the measure as well as a strength. While the label may survive intact from year to year, the meaning associated with it may change considerably over time. If parties have become less relevant to the public in recent decades, as I argue, then opinions about the parties may have dissipated even among those whose party labels remain intact.

The best test for this hypothesis is to compare the frequency of a neutral response to the party like/dislike questions over time, controlling for strength of party identification. The following comparison of the level of neutrality toward the parties in 1952 and 1992 reveals an increase for each level of strength of party identification:

	1952	1992
Strong party identifiers	5%	15%
Weak party identifiers	15%	31%
Independent leaners	12%	37%
Pure Independents	23%	59%

Thus strength of party identification no longer has the depth of meaning it once did. The significance of the rise of neutrality is not so much that it partially explains the decline of party identification as that it indicates an even sharper decline in party relevance than the rise in the percentage of Independents would lead us to expect.

Another indicator of the irrelevance of political parties to many Americans can be found in their responses to the question of which party would do a better job of handling the most important problem facing the country. Once again, only about half of the survey respondents felt that either the Democrats or the Republicans would do a better job in 1992 (see the last segment of Table 10.1). And as noted in the previous chapter, while the proportion of people who believe there are important differences in what the parties stand for has risen recently, this has not led to any corresponding increase in the belief that parties can make a difference when it comes to solving problems.[16]

When George Wallace garnered 13.5 percent of the vote in 1968, one of his most frequent sayings was that "there's not a dime's worth of difference between the two parties." Ross Perot's even more successful independent candidacy focused more on the criticism that neither party was offering a viable solution to the budget deficit and other pressing problems. Perot thus attempted to capitalize on the perceived irrelevance of parties more than any other candidate in recent history. As will be seen in the next section, lack of partisanship was indeed strongly related to voting for Perot.

Analyzing the Perot Vote

In many important ways, those who voted for Ross Perot represented a virtual cross-section of the American electorate. As can be seen from the exit poll results in Table 10.2, Perot made substantial inroads among most all social and political groups.[17] Whereas Clinton and Bush attracted voters from specific political and economic groups, Perot attracted a more

Table 10.2   How political and social groups voted in 1992 (in percentages)

	Clinton	Bush	Perot
Democrats	78	10	13
Independents	39	31	30
Republicans	11	72	18
Liberals	69	13	18
Moderates	49	30	21
Conservatives	18	64	17
Whites	40	39	21
African-Americans	83	11	7
Hispanics	62	24	14
Women	47	36	17
Men	41	37	21
Married	40	40	20
Unmarried	49	33	18
White born-again Christians	23	61	15
Catholics	42	37	21
Jews	78	10	11
18–29 years old	44	34	22
30–44	42	38	20
45–59	41	40	19
60 and over	50	37	12
Family income under $15,000	59	22	19
$15,000–29,999	46	34	20
$30,000–$49,999	42	37	21
$50,000–$74,999	41	41	18
Over $75,000	38	46	16
Union households	56	23	22

SOURCE: Voter Research and Surveys exit poll.

diverse set of supporters. For example, voters with incomes over $75,000 a year gave 24 percent more of their votes to President Bush than those with incomes under $15,000. Perot managed to get 16 percent of the vote of those in the highest income bracket while at the same time getting 19 percent from those in the lowest income category. Along political lines, liberals were 51 percent more likely than conservatives to cast their vote for Clinton but just 1 percent more likely to vote for Perot.

The lack of a clear ideological or social base of support for Ross Perot fits with his campaign's nontraditional approach. American politicians usually follow a building-block strategy, seeking support from different groups in order to form a winning coalition. But Perot studiously avoided a strategy of appealing to various economic and social interests. After all, Perot adamantly maintained that much of what was wrong with American government was the inordinate power of special interest groups. Ironically, the only time Perot ventured into the world of interest group politics it backfired on him. His address to the National Association for the Advancement of Colored Persons revealed insensitivities to the concerns of African-Americans. Interestingly, African-Americans were the only group identified in the exit poll that gave Perot less than 10 percent of their vote.[18]

As might be expected from his nonpartisan stance, Perot did best with Independents, who gave him 30 percent of their vote. *The Myth of the Independent Voter* concludes "Since Independents are so diverse, it is difficult to imagine them rallying behind a major third party offering any alternative set of policies."[19] Yet rally behind Ross Perot in disproportionate numbers they did, despite their differences on the issues.

Perhaps the best indicator of the Perot supporters' diversity is what they said they would have done had Perot not been on the ballot. In the nationwide exit poll, 38 percent said they would have voted for Clinton, 37 percent for Bush, 6 percent for other candidates, and 15 percent said they would not have voted.[20] Similarly, the National Election Study data show that Perot voters were just 4 percent more likely to prefer Bush to Clinton, as measured by feeling thermometer ratings. In contrast, in 1968 Wallace voters preferred Nixon over Humphrey by a margin of 40 percent, and in 1980 Anderson voters preferred Carter over Reagan by 21 percent.[21] Unlike the Wallace and Anderson voters, the Perot voters did not represent a breakaway group from either the Democratic or the Republican coalition.

What the Perot voters had most in common was lack of partisan attachment, which made them open to voting for a previously unknown candidate with no experience in elected office. The less attached an individual was to a political party, the more likely he or she was to vote for Perot. In order to demonstrate this, I have constructed a partisanship scale that employs four dimensions of attitudes about parties, each of which adds to the ability to predict the Perot vote. These four dimensions are:

1. Affiliative, as measured by identification with a party or not.
2. Cognitive, employing the pattern of responses to

the open-ended questions about the parties. A positive-negative pattern was coded as partisan whereas a neutral-neutral pattern was coded as nonpartisan. Other patterns were not counted as either partisan or nonpartisan.

3. Affective, using the feeling thermometer ratings of the parties and the same coding conventions as the cognitive dimension.

4. Performance, in which those who said there would be a difference between the parties in handling the nation's most important problem were coded as partisan and those who saw no difference or didn't know were coded as nonpartisan.

By subtracting the number of nonpartisan responses from the number of partisan responses, a multi-faceted partisanship scale is created ranging from −4 to +4. As can be seen in Table 10.3, the relationship between the partisanship scale and voting for Perot is fairly strong and distinctly linear until one reaches the sparsely populated "least partisan" category.

Yet the vote for Perot was limited by the odd nature of the candidate himself. Ed Rollins, his one-time campaign manager, wrote in a prominent op-ed piece, "In my first meeting with Ross Perot in June, I wrote two words on a blackboard: 'hope' and 'kook.' I told him that for him to win, he would have to cast himself as the agent of hope. I also told him that every day, the Republicans and Democrats would attempt to cast him as a kook. Little did I know no one could make him look more kooky than he has himself."[22] Befitting the unpredictable nature of the candidate, no discernable patterns are evident in the survey data regarding

Table 10.3 Percent voting for Perot by partisanship index

		All voters	Voters rating Perot positively
Most Partisan	+4	5.2% (232)	10.9% (101)
	+3	8.0% (200)	18.8% (80)
	+2	16.2% (278)	30.2% (129)
	+1	19.3% (296)	34.3% (143)
	0	21.7% (230)	43.0% (107)
	−1	24.7% (174)	44.7% (85)
	−2	26.4% (129)	46.3% (67)
	−3	38.0% (92)	67.3% (49)
Least Partisan	−4	33.3% (27)	61.5% (13)

NOTE: The partisanship index is calculated by subtracting the number of nonpartisan attitudes from the number of partisan attitudes for four variables. The following list shows how each variable was coded:

	Coded as nonpartisan	Coded as partisan
party identification	Independent	Democrat or Republican
most important problem	no party difference, don't know	Democrat or Republican
feeling thermometers	neutral-neutral pattern	positive-negative pattern
likes/dislikes	neutral-neutral pattern	positive-negative pattern

SOURCE: 1992 National Election Study.

who viewed Perot favorably. Whether one thought he was crazy (Perot himself adopted "Crazy" as his theme song) or a welcome alternative appears to have been a matter of strictly individual judgment, unaffected by political predispositions.

Most important for the purposes of this analysis, it can be calculated from the number of cases in each row of Table 10.3 that there was virtually no relationship between the strength of partisanship index and rating Perot favorably on the feeling thermometer. Therefore, one constraint on the relationship between the Perot vote and the partisanship strength scale is simply that many of those who were quite open to an independent candidate just did not like the Texas businessman. Once one controls for whether voters felt positively toward Perot (the second column of Table 10.3), the relationship improves substantially.

Three decades ago, Philip Converse and Georges Dupeux argued that voters are less likely to be attracted to flash parties and demagogic leaders when many citizens feel strongly attached to established political parties.[23] Examining the behavior of voters in the two most strongly partisan categories who liked Perot offers a good example of how partisan attachments can insulate voters from flash candidates. Of these voters, only 14 percent decided actually to cast their ballots for him. In contrast, over 60 percent of the people who liked Perot in the two least partisan categories were swept along with the short-term tide.

If Perot decides to run for president again in 1996, he will no longer be a flash in the pan (though many will no doubt continue to call him a demagogue). Perot's initial jump into the political arena may have been sudden, but in the year following the 1992 election he has taken on the role of opposition spokesman, a role no losing presidential candidate has attempted to perform since Adlai Stevenson in the 1950s. Rather than dropping out of the public eye, like so many recent failed presidential candidates, Perot has continued to speak out on the issues of the day through talk shows, media events, thirty-minute TV infomercials, and an unprecedented TV debate with Al Gore. Rarely specific regarding what he would do if he were president, he has offered a running critique of President Clinton's actions and proposals, establishing himself as the most visible center of opposition to the President.

One feature of the British party model that has long appealed to many American observers is the weekly sparring between the prime minister and the leader of the opposition. The continual give-and-take between the party leaders provides British voters with a good sense of the difference between what the government is doing and what the opposition might do if it were in power. The staying power of Ross Perot after the 1992 election has given American voters at least some of the flavor of such debates, though without the formalized process of the British model.

What most distinguishes Perot's exchanges with Clinton and Gore from parliamentary debate is the lack of a political party standing behind Perot. His political career up to this point has been a classic demonstration of the candidate-centered nature of modern American politics. Even Theodore Lowi, a prominent political scientist who published a call for Perot to found a third party,[24] has criticized this Lone Ranger aspect of Perot's behavior: "If he'd won, it would have been the worst thing that could have happened. Talk about deadlock! With not a single member of his own party in Congress!"[25] Similarly, Dan Quayle remarked in June 1992 that "electing Ross Perot wouldn't fix the deadlock between the elected branches—it would make this worse."[26] Later in the campaign, Quayle went so far as to suggest, "If you're going to vote for Bill Clinton, I'd say vote for your Democratic congressman . . . It's a controversial viewpoint, and it's not shared by all the people in my party. But I think we must end the divided government."[27]

With Clinton winning the presidency and the Democrats maintaining control of both houses of Congress, the era of divided party government has come to at least a temporary end. In the wake of the recent extended period of split presidential-congressional control, a good deal of research has been produced on the causes and consequences of divided government. One of the most important by-products of party decline, it merits attention before I close this chapter.

Party Decline and Divided Government

According to Morris Fiorina, "divided government has the potential to become the new organizing principle of American politics research in the 1990s."[28] Although unified party government has now been restored at the national level, evidence from the state governments indicates that divided party government remains an important phenomenon in American politics. The percentage of states which have unified party control of the governorship and the state legislature has steadily declined for over four decades. In 1947, 85 percent of state governments had one party controlling both houses of the legislature and the governorship, but by 1993 this was the case in only 40 percent of the states. Divided government, once an oddity, is now commonplace.

One possible reason why voters regularly split control between the parties may be to limit the parties' power. The Founding Fathers designed the Constitution so that no one faction would have too much power. Yet the formation of political parties made it possible to overcome some of the constraints of the Madisonian system of checks and balances. By splitting control of the elected branches between the parties, voters thus make the system work as the founders intended.

Another frequently cited reason for ticket-splitting is a lack of voter confidence in either party. As Fiorina has hypothesized, "consciously or unconsciously, some small but important portion of the electorate is engaging in a kind of sophisticated ticket-splitting that permits them to register a preference for a middle course between two parties, neither of which they fully trust to govern."[29]

Over the last few years, the question of whether voters would rather see unified or divided party government has been asked in several ways, yielding conflicting survey results.[30] Probably the best-worded question can be found in the 1992 National Election Study, which asked respondents, "Do you think it is better when one party controls both the presidency and Congress, better when control is split between the Democrats and Republicans, or doesn't it matter?" Of

those who voted for President and the House, 35 percent preferred unified party control, 38 percent fa-
vored divided party control, 25 percent said it didn't
matter, and 2 percent said they didn't know. Thus
there were enough voters who preferred divided government for Fiorina's theory to prove valid—providing that they actually account for a disproportionate
share of ticket-splitters. This was not the case in 1992.
Those voters who thought it would be better to split
partisan control were only 3 percent more likely than
average to cast a vote for one party's presidential candidate for President and the House candidate from the
other party.[31]

People who split their tickets may not be latter-day
Madisonians, wishing to constrain government, but
instead may want to have their cake and eat it too.
Gary Jacobson argues that more Democrats are sent to
Congress because they are perceived as being the most
capable of reaping the benefits of government for the
district, whereas Republicans are generally elected to
the presidency in order to hold the line on taxes and
federal spending: "There is nothing irrational here; we
naturally enjoy the benefits government confers but
dislike paying for them."[32] Similarly, John Petrocik
puts forth a theory of issue ownership which argues
that issues such as taxes and defense help
Republicans win nationally oriented presidential
elections whereas social service issues help the
Democrats win locally oriented congressional races.[33]
According to this theory, American voters have effec-
tively chosen not to choose between the parties.
Rather than frustrating public opinion, divided government can thus be seen as actually reflecting it.

An alternative reason why voters may split their ticket is not so much the parties' different appeals but rather that people don't think their performances will be different. As can be seen from Table 10.4, the percentage that does not believe that one party would do a better job than the other numbered at least 30 percent on all the issues asked about in 1992. And without the stimulus of a presidential election in 1990, a majority said there would be no difference in the parties' performance on each of the issues.

Nevertheless, the pattern of Democrats doing better on social welfare issues and Republicans on foreign affairs is apparent in the data for both years. For example, 21 percent of all 1992 voters thought the Republicans would do the best job on foreign affairs whereas the Democrats would handle health care best. According to the theory of issue ownership, these voters would be particularly likely to split their tickets. However, they were actually about 2 percent less likely than the total electorate to vote for Bush and for their Democratic House candidate. A more elaborate test of the theory can be achieved by counting the number of pro-Democrat and pro-Republican performance responses in order to identify people who usually believe that parties produce different results but see a tradeoff between them. About one-fifth of all voters believed there were party differences on the majority of the questions and gave an equal number of pro-Democrat and pro-Republican responses or a split verdict of either 3–2 or 2–1. Of these voters, the likelihood of splitting their House and presidential vote between the two parties was only 2 percent greater than for the total electorate.

Table 10.4 Assessments of which party would do a better job, 1990 and 1992

Problem	No difference, don't know	Democrats	Republicans
1992			
Handling the nation's economy	43	37	20
Handling foreign affairs	33	22	45
Solving the problem of poverty	38	51	11
Making health care more affordable	34	54	12
Keeping out of war	62	20	18
1990			
Handling the nation's economy	60	20	20
Handling the problem of pollution and protection of the environment	60	30	10
Dealing with the crime problem	69	15	17
Handling foreign affairs	57	15	28
Cleaning up the savings and loan business	66	23	11

NOTE: The wording of the question is as follows: "Which party do you think would do a better job of ———, the Democrats, the Republicans, or wouldn't there be much difference between them?"

SOURCE: 1990 and 1992 National Election Studies.

In contrast to the notion of issue ownership, this book's emphasis on the declining relevance of political parties would predict that ticket-splitters are those who generally see "no difference" between the parties' issue performance. Indeed, a significant linear relationship is found between ticket-splitting and the number of "no difference" responses on the party performance questions. Rather than ticket-splitting being caused by the different appeals of the parties, it is the lack of perceived partisan advantages that opens the way for people to split their tickets.

A major fault with both the intentional ticket-splitting and issue ownership theories is that they depend on political parties being important to the voters who are most responsible for dividing power between the parties. Fiorina rightly notes that "party decline is a precondition rather than an explanation"[34] for divided government, but any explanation must rely on factors that could only become more important in an era of weakened partisanship. Incumbency, for example, would not be as important a factor in maintaining Democratic control of the House if political parties were as strong as they used to be. Nor would it be possible for the party with the most voter identification regularly to lose presidential elections.

In an era of weakened political parties, characteristics of individual candidates become increasingly important. The task of explaining why divided party government occurs therefore becomes one of identifying why candidate factors tend to favor the Democrats in legislative races and the Republicans in presidential races. On the legislative side, a good deal of work points in the same direction—that the Democratic

Party has simply been more successful at nominating candidates capable of mounting a strong campaign. Gary Jacobson's analysis shows that Democrats have consistently fielded a higher percentage of experienced House nominees—defined as those who have held some sort of prior elected office.[35] Furthermore, he demonstrates that experienced candidates of both parties are much more likely to be victorious. Why the Republicans are at a recruiting disadvantage for the House is a difficult question. Alan Ehrenhalt argues that today's entrepreneurial politics foster candidates who are committed to looking after local constituents, getting as much from the government for them as they can.[36] Such a job description conflicts with the view of many Republicans that government is the source of the nation's problems rather than the solution to them. The Democrats' general belief in government as an instrument to advance society gives them an edge in putting forward experienced candidates for legislative office.

In the race for the presidency, establishing which party benefits from candidate factors is more complex, as virtually all nominees have extensive experience. Republican nominees have enjoyed a structural advantage in the era of weakened partisanship, since the Democrats' reformed nomination process has made it difficult for Democratic candidates to emerge with sufficient party unity to win in November.[37] Somewhat paradoxically, the decline of partisanship has made party unity more important than ever. The party label is no longer sufficient to pull various factions back together after a bitter nomination fight.

There are two basic reasons why the Republicans

have generally been able to achieve greater party unity in presidential campaigns. First, since the Goldwater wing took over the Republican Party in 1964 the GOP has been more ideologically cohesive. Compared to the Democrats, Republican presidential contenders have had relatively little cause to engage in bitter policy disputes. The existence of markedly different constituencies has given Democratic presidential candidates much more to fight about in the primaries.

Second, more often than not, the Republicans suffer less from the potential divisiveness of primary campaigns due to their greater use of winner-take-all delegation selection rules. For example, in 1988 the Republicans selected roughly three-fifths of their delegates in this fashion, the Democrats only about one-fifth of their delegates.[38] The winner-take-all method offers little incentive for losing candidates to continue divisive nomination campaigns. In contrast, strict adherence to proportional representation in most Democratic primaries fosters "Timex" candidates—candidates who "take a licking and keep on ticking." The significance of a protracted nomination campaign is illustrated by the fact that the candidate who wrapped up his party's nomination fastest and with the least bitterness won every presidential election from 1964 to 1988.

It is less clear which party had this advantage in 1992. President Bush was the first to accumulate the necessary delegates to ensure the Republican nomination, but by this point Bill Clinton was considered to have the Democratic nomination locked up. Winning a majority of delegates did not end Bush's internal party problems. Republican candidate Patrick J.

Buchanan managed to win 26 percent of the vote in the California primary, thereby demonstrating continued Republican dissatisfaction with Bush. Most important, Buchanan's stridently conservative speech at the GOP convention showed the open fissures in the party, whereas the Democratic convention succeeded in rallying the party around Clinton. The opinion polls showed no post-convention bounce for Bush, compared to a substantial leap for Clinton. In the end, Republicans were less likely to vote for their party's nominee than Democrats. Despite closing the gap in party identification during the 1980s, the GOP remained the minority party and hence could not prevail without being more united than the Democrats.[39]

Why did the advantage of party unity turn in favor of the Democrats in 1992? Part of the answer is that for once the Republicans had a serious policy disagreement. Buchanan's challenge of Bush would have proven no more fruitful than Ashbrook's 1972 challenge of Nixon had Bush not angered many Republicans by reneging on his "no new taxes" pledge. A majority of House Republicans failed to support the compromise budget proposal that Bush worked out with the Democrats. Buchanan was merely a manifestation of this deeply rooted division within the GOP in 1992.

When Bill Clinton became the apparent Democratic nominee in March he remarked, "I have always believed that Democrats often forfeit the November election by the nature of the primary process, and I've worked very, very hard to keep that from happening this time."[40] More than any action on Clinton's part, however, it was the inaction of other candidates that made 1992 different for the Democrats. Ironically, the fact that no nationally prominent Democratic leader ran for the presidency in 1992 opened the way for the least bitter and protracted nomination struggle the party had seen since the nomination process was reformed. Had candidates with strong financial backing and an established constituency—such as Mario Cuomo or Richard Gephardt—decided to run, the primary battles would almost certainly have been more intense. A struggle between Democratic heavyweights would probably have left the party far more divided and enabled the Republicans to retain their usual advantage in party unity.

The return of united party government has given the parties, particularly the Democrats, a good chance to demonstrate their relevance to the American public. Having one party control both the presidency and the Congress may not affect the amount of major legislation passed per session, as David Mayhew shows.[41] However, it surely makes it easier for citizens to assess accountability for the government's performance. As James Sundquist writes, "When a single party has responsibility for both branches, the people in their one sovereign act—the act of voting—can render a verdict and thus set the general direction of governmental policy."[42]

Such a theoretical possibility depends on the public's focusing on parties as opposed to personalities. The continued prominence of Ross Perot on the political scene works against this. Perot's nonstop campaign against Clinton, which the media has focused upon, has once again pushed partisanship off the political stage. Although Clinton depended even more than Reagan on his own party's members in Congress for passage of his economic program, the program has been similarly personalized. Rather than "Democratic economics," the media almost always use the phrase "Clintonomics." And even though Congressional Republicans were extraordinarily united in opposition to this program, they have received less than the opposition's usual share of attention. Just when the Republicans are well positioned to capitalize on any mishaps on the Democrats' watch, it is not the GOP but rather Ross Perot who is the focal point of opposition. One major reason for this is that there is no agreement regarding who is the leader of the Republican Party. There is no doubt who heads the Perot movement.

In addition to diverting attention away from the Republicans, there is evidence that Perot has the potential to draw votes away from them as well. Among voters in 1992 who felt positively toward Perot but did not vote for him, over three-fifths cast their ballots for Bush. Should a more established Perot improve his showing at the polls in 1996, the gain will likely come disproportionately out of the Republican column. If Ross Perot continues to be a substantial independent force on the political scene, it will be quite a demonstration of the decline of American political parties. With or without Perot, there will likely be further manifestations of party decline in the years to come.

Notes

Introduction

1. E. E. Schattschneider, *Party Government* (New York: Farrar and Rinehart, 1942), p. 1.
2. David S. Broder, *The Party's Over: The Failure of Politics in America* (New York: Harper and Row, 1971), p. xxiii.
3. Morris P. Fiorina, "The Decline of Collective Responsibility in American Politics," *Daedalus* 109 (1980): 44.
4. Malcolm E. Jewell and David M. Olson, *American State Political Parties and Elections*, rev. ed. (Homewood, Ill.: Dorsey, 1982).
5. Cornelius Cotter and John F. Bibby, "Institutional Development of Parties and the Thesis of Party Decline," *Political Science Quarterly* 95 (1980): 1–27.
6. Austin Ranney, "The Political Parties: Reform and Decline," in Anthony King, ed., *The New American Political System* (Washington, D.C.: American Enterprise Institute, 1978), p. 215.
7. S. E. Finer, *The Changing British Party System, 1945–1979* (Washington, D.C.: American Enterprise Institute, 1980), p. xii.

1. The Concept of Political Partisanship

1. Jack Dennis, "Some Properties of Measures of Partisanship" (paper presented at the annual meeting of the American Political Science Association, 1981), p. 4.

2. See Paul Lazarfeld, Bernard Berelson, and Hazel Gaudet, *The People's Choice* (New York: Columbia University Press, 1944); and Bernard Berelson, Paul Lazarfeld, and William McPhee, *Voting: A Study of Opinion Formation in a Presidential Campaign* (Chicago: University of Chicago Press, 1954).

3. See Ian Budge, Ivor Crewe, and Dennis Fairlie, eds., *Party Identification and Beyond* (New York: Wiley, 1975).

4. See Philip E. Converse, "The Concept of a Normal Vote," in Angus Campbell et al., *Elections and the Political Order* (New York: Wiley, 1966); and Arthur H. Miller, "Normal Vote Analysis: Sensitivity to Change over Time," *American Journal of Political Science* 23, (1979): 406–423.

5. Party affiliation here has been defined as loosely as possible by including Independent leaners with the identifiers of each party. If one excludes these leaners, then only 2 percent of the 1972–1976 voters can be said to have shifted their identification from one party to the other between the two presidential elections.

6. Philip E. Converse and Georges Dupeux, "Politicalization of the Electorate in France and the United States," in Campbell et al., *Elections and the Political Order.*

7. Angus Campbell, Gerald Gurin, and Warren E. Miller, *The Voter Decides* (Evanston, Ill.: Row, Peterson, 1954), p. 90.

8. Angus Campbell, Philip E. Converse, Warren E. Miller, and Donald E. Stokes, *The American Voter* (New York: Wiley, 1960), p. 121.

9. Warren E. Miller, "The Cross-National Use of Party Identification as a Stimulus to Political Inquiry," in Budge, Crewe, and Fairlie, eds., *Party Identification and Beyond,* p. 22.

10. See Richard A. Brody and Benjamin I. Page, "Comment:

The Assessment of Policy Voting," *American Political Science Review* 66 (1972): 450–458; and Gregory B. Markus and Philip E. Converse, "A Dynamic Simultaneous Model of Electoral Choice," *American Political Science Review* 73 (1979): 406–423.

11. See Richard W. Boyd, "Decline of U.S. Voter Turnout: Structural Explanations," *American Politics Quarterly* 9 (1981): 133–159.

12. Anthony Downs, *An Economic Theory of Democracy* (New York: Harper and Row, 1957), p. 233.

13. Warren E. Miller and Donald E. Stokes, "Constituency Influence in Congress," in Campbell et al., *Elections and the Political Order*.

14. Morris P. Fiorina, *Retrospective Voting in American National Elections* (New Haven, Conn.: Yale University Press, 1981), pp. 89–90.

15. See Richard A. Brody, "Stability and Change in Party Identification: Presidential to Off-Years" (paper presented at the annual meeting of the American Political Science Association, 1977); and Gregory B. Markus, "The Political Environment and the Dynamics of Public Attitudes: A Panel Study," *American Journal of Political Science* 23 (1979): 338–359.

16. Charles H. Franklin and John E. Jackson, "The Dynamics of Party Identification" (paper presented at the annual meeting of the American Political Science Association, 1981), p. 18.

17. Herbert F. Weisberg, "A Multidimensional Conceptualization of Party Identification," *Political Behavior* 2 (1980): 33–60.

18. Jack Dennis, "Trends in Public Support for the American Party System," *British Journal of Political Science* 5 (1975): 230.

19. See Richard Hofstadter, *The Idea of a Party System* (Berkeley: University of California Press, 1969); and Austin Ranney, *Curing the Mischiefs of Faction: Party Reform in America* (Berkeley: University of California Press, 1975), chapter 2.

20. Walter Dean Burnham, *Critical Elections and the Mainsprings of American Politics* (New York: Norton, 1970).

21. One other possible problem concerns the decline of regionalism in party identification. When the distribution of partisanship in a district approaches an even split between Democrats and Republicans, as it has throughout the South and elsewhere, the level of ticket-splitting necessary to cause a split outcome declines. In other words, the same degree of individual-level ticket-splitting could theoretically be responsible for a substantially higher number of split outcomes.

22. Warren E. Miller and Teresa E. Levitan, *Leadership and Change: The New Politics and the American Electorate* (Cambridge, Mass.: Winthrop, 1976).

23. Patrick H. Caddell, "The Democratic Strategy and Its Electoral Consequences," in Seymour Martin Lipset, ed., *Party Coalitions in the 1980s* (San Francisco: Institute for Contemporary Studies, 1981), p. 300.

24. Dennis, "Trends in Public Support."

25. Converse, "The Concept of a Normal Vote."

26. Philip E. Converse, *The Dynamics of Party Support: Cohort-Analyzing Party Identification* (Beverly Hills, Calif.: Sage Publications, 1976).

27. Burnham, *Critical Elections*, pp. 130–131.

28. Gerald Pomper, "Impacts on the Political System," in Samuel Kirkpatrick, ed., *American Electoral Behavior: Change and Stability* (Beverly Hills, Calif.: Sage Publications, 1976), p. 137.

29. See Converse, *The Dynamics of Party Support*, pp. 106–111, for a lively discussion of these shocks.

30. Bruce Keith et al., "The Myth of the Independent Voter" (paper presented at the annual meeting of the American Political Science Association, 1977).

31. For the figures for each year individually see Warren E. Miller, "Policy Directions and Presidential Leadership: Alternative Interpretations of the 1980 Presidential Election" (paper presented at the annual meeting of the American Political Science Association, 1981).

32. Keith et al., "The Myth of the Independent Voter," p. 3.

33. Philip E. Converse and Gregory B. Markus, "Plus ça change . . . : The New CPS Election Study Panel," *American Political Science Review* 73 (1979): 32–49.

34. Philip E. Converse, "The Nature of Belief Systems in Mass Publics," in David E. Apter, ed., *Ideology and Discontent* (Glencoe, Ill.: Free Press, 1964).

35. Converse and Markus, "Plus ça change," p. 45.

36. See John A. Ferejohn, "On the Decline of Competition in Congressional Elections," *American Political Science Review* 71 (1977): 166–176; and Norman H. Nie, Sidney Verba, and John R. Petrocik, *The Changing American Voter* (Cambridge, Mass.: Harvard University Press, 1976).

2. The Stability of Partisan Attitudes

1. See David C. Valentine and John R. Van Wingen, "Partisanship, Independence, and the Partisan Identification Question," *American Politics Quarterly* 8 (1980): 165–186; Weisberg, "A Multidimensional Conceptualization of Party Identification"; and Dennis, "Some Properties of Measures of Partisanship."

2. Samuel J. Eldersveld, "The Independent Vote: Measurement, Characteristics and Implications for Party Strategy," *American Political Science Review* 46 (1952): 752.

3. Campbell et al., *The American Voter*, p. 144.

4. Christopher H. Achen, "Mass Political Attitudes and the Survey Response," *American Political Science Review* 69 (1975): 1218–31.

5. Since only three responses were coded to each question in the 1972 wave of the '72–'76 panel the indices in both panels have been constructed on the basis of the first three responses. The range of each index is thus from +3 to −3.

3. Independent or No Preference?

1. See Paul A. Abramson, "Generational Change and the Decline of Party Identification in America: 1952–1974," *Ameri-*

can Political Science Review 70 (1976): 469–478; and Converse, *The Dynamics of Party Support.*

2. See Campbell et al., *The American Voter;* Burnham, *Critical Elections;* Gerald Pomper, *Voter's Choice: Varieties of American Electoral Behavior* (New York: Dodd, Mead, 1975); and Herbert B. Asher, *Presidential Elections and American Politics,* 2d edition (Homewood, Ill.: Dorsey, 1980).

3. See John R. Petrocik, "An Analysis of the Intransitivities of Party Identification," *Political Methodology* 1 (1974): 31–47; Brody, "Stability and Change"; Keith et al., "The Myth of the Independent Voter"; and W. Philips Shively, "Information Costs and the Partisan Life Cycle" (paper presented at the annual meeting of the American Political Science Association, 1977).

4. Converse, *The Dynamics of Party Support,* p. 127.

5. In 1980 this procedure was standardized and documented for the first time. As stated in the codebook for the study, respondents were coded as apoliticals only if they showed little or no interest in response to questions regarding their interest in the campaign, concern about which party would win, intention to vote, and general attention to politics.

6. Since 1968 the responses to each of the questions in the party identification series have been coded separately in each dataset. Therefore, one can easily identify those people who initially say that they have "no preference" on the basis of the coded responses to the lead question. However, before 1968 only the traditional derived scale was coded. Thus I returned to the original interview protocols to obtain this information for 1964.

7. The analysis in this chapter begins with 1964 because it marks the last election year in Converse's steady-state period of strength of partisanship. Earlier years would therefore look much the same in all probability.

8. This change was not an artifact of lowering the voting age to eighteen in 1972, as the shift is virtually the same when those aged eighteen to twenty are excluded.

9. Because of the small number of cases in some years for

some of the categories, pooling the data from these five studies provides far more reliable estimates. There are of course some fluctuations from year to year, but the basic patterns are found consistently in each study.

10. In order to increase the sample size for these figures I have combined data from the P1, C1, and C3 waves of the 1980 study.

11. One plausible explanation for these patterns may be that as those with no preference are less politically involved than Independents, they will be more likely to agree with any statement in an interview situation. However, when other agree-disagree items are examined such a hypothesis is not confirmed.

4. Negativity or Neutrality?

1. Nie, Verba, and Petrocik, *The Changing American Voter,* pp. 57–58.

2. Kristi Andersen, "Generation, Partisan Shift, and Realignment: A Glance Back to the New Deal," in Nie, Verba, and Petrocik, *The Changing American Voter,* p. 95.

3. James L. Sundquist, *Dynamics of the Party System: Alignment and Realignment of Political Parties in the United States* (Washington, D.C.: The Brookings Institution, 1973), p. 353.

4. Nie, Verba, and Petrocik, *The Changing American Voter,* p. 283.

5. The wording of this question has changed slightly over the years. Listed below are the different versions that have been asked:

1952: "Do you think there are any important differences between what the Democratic and Republican parties stand for, or do you think they are about the same?"

1960, 1964, 1972–1980: "Do you think there are any important differences in what the Republicans and Democrats stand for?"

1968: "Do you think there are any important differences between the Republican and Democratic parties?"

6. This question has also undergone slight changes in wording over the years. In 1960, 1964 and 1968 respondents were asked which party they thought would be the most likely to do what they wanted on whichever problem they mentioned. In 1972 this was changed to asking which party would be the most likely to get the government to be helpful on the problem, and in 1976–1980 the wording was again changed to which party would be the most likely to do a better job in dealing with the problem.

7. Merle Black and George B. Rabinowitz, "American Electoral Change: 1952–1972 (with a note on 1976)," in William Crotty, ed., *The Party Symbol: Readings on Political Parties* (San Francisco: W. H. Freeman, 1980), p. 241.

8. I wish to thank M. Kent Jennings for making these data available to me, as well as for offering advice concerning their use.

9. See Abramson, "Generational Change."

10. Sundquist, *Dynamics of the Party System*, p. 343.

11. In 1972 CPS originally coded only the first three responses. The fourth and fifth responses were later coded by Arthur H. Miller. I wish to thank Professor Miller for making these data available to me.

12. Several technical differences between the like/dislike data that I have used and those that Nie et al. use should be noted. First, Nie et al. use only the first three responses in all years while I employ all five. Second, they fail to filter out the 100 respondents in 1952 and the 17 in 1960 who were not interviewed in the preelection wave. As these respondents were not asked the like/dislike questions they should be excluded from the analysis. Finally, Nie et al. include responses from the Black supplements in 1964 and 1968. Subsequent analysis at CPS has shown that these supplements actually introduce a greater degree of bias into the sample. Hence I have not used them.

13. The proportion without any positive or negative com-

ments for each year are as follows: 1952, 9.7%; 1956, 12.9%; 1960, 15.7%; 1964, 17.1%; 1968, 14.0%; 1972, 27.0%; 1976, 28.7%; 1980, 34.3%. The tiny remainder of those who fall under the neutral-neutral category in Table 4.4 express both likes and dislikes, with each like being matched by a dislike of the same party.

14. In the 1964 and 1968 studies those who responded "don't know" were coded at the 50 degree mark. Therefore, I have followed the same coding rule with the 1972–1980 data to ensure consistency throughout the time series.

15. Furthermore, there are two reasons to expect that this jump may be a methodological artifact of changes in the structure of the interview schedule in 1980. First, respondents were also asked to rate the "Democratic Party" and the "Republican Party" in the preelection interview. And second, the preelection interview in 1980 focused more on political parties than any other in the past. Both of these factors could well have caused respondents to think more about the parties than they would have otherwise and therefore rate them less neutrally. The reason such an effect is not found in the like/dislike questions is that these remained very early in the preelection interview whereas the 1980 feeling thermometer ratings shown in Table 4.5 are from the postelection wave.

16. Similarly, when asked which party would do a better job in handling inflation, only 42 percent of those interviewed in 1980 thought one party would do a better job than the other, and regarding unemployment the comparable figure was just 39 percent.

5. Political Leadership and the Parties

1. Campbell et al., *The American Voter*, p. 318.

2. Lester G. Seligman, "The Presidential Office and the President as Party Leader (with a Postscript on the Kennedy-Nixon Era)," in Jeff Fishel, ed., *Parties and Elections in an Anti-Party Age* (Bloomington: Indiana University Press, 1978), p. 300.

3. Schattschneider, *Party Government*, p. 64.

4. Donald M. Fraser, "Democratizing the Democratic Party," in Robert A. Goldwin, ed., *Political Parties in the Eighties* (Washington, D.C.: American Enterprise Institute), p. 129.

5. See Ranney, *Curing the Mischiefs of Faction;* William Crotty, *Political Reform and the American Experiment* (New York: Crowell, 1977); and Jeane J. Kirkpatrick, *Dismantling the Parties: Reflections on Party Reform and Party Decomposition* (Washington, D.C.: American Enterprise Institute, 1978).

6. See William R. Keech and Donald R. Matthews, *The Party's Choice* (Washington, D.C.: The Brookings Institution, 1976).

7. Barbara G. Farah, "Convention Delegates: Party Reform and the Representatives of Party Elites, 1972–1980" (paper presented at the annual meeting of the American Political Science Association, 1981).

8. See Thomas E. Patterson, *The Mass Media Election: How Americans Choose Their President* (New York: Praeger, 1980).

9. Ranney, "The Political Parties," p. 239.

10. Thomas E. Cronin, *The State of the Presidency,* 2d ed. (Boston: Little, Brown, 1980), p. 246.

11. Hugh Heclo, "The Changing Presidential Office," in Arnold J. Meltsner, ed., *Politics and the Oval Office* (San Francisco: Institute for Contemporary Studies, 1981), pp. 168–169.

12. Morris P. Fiorina, *Congress: Keystone of the Washington Establishment* (New Haven, Conn.: Yale University Press, 1977).

13. See Nie, Verba, and Petrocik, *The Changing American Voter,* pp. 55–57.

14. The candidate evaluation data were originally gathered as part of a research project undertaken by Arthur H. Miller, who kindly granted me permission to use them. The dimensions of the party like/dislike questions have been constructed precisely according to the subheadings in the election study codebooks. The same is true for the candidate dimensions with the exception of that of general philosophy. Most of the

codes in this dimension can be found between 805 and 828 in the 1972 and 1976 codebooks. The distinction between responses on this dimension and those on domestic and foreign policy is that the former deals only with broad comments such as liberal, conservative, humanistic, anti–states' rights, pro–big government, and so on.

15. Quoted in Broder, *The Party's Over*, p. 6.

16. See Arthur H. Miller and Martin P. Wattenberg, "Policy and Performance Voting in the 1980 Election" (paper presented at the annual meeting of the American Political Science Association, 1981).

6. The Role of the Media

1. Robert Agranoff, *The Management of Electoral Campaigns* (Boston: Holbrook Press, 1976).

2. Fiorina, "The Decline of Collective Responsibility," p. 33.

3. Frank J. Sorauf, *Party Politics in America*, 4th ed. (Boston: Little, Brown and Co., 1980), p. 255.

4. Sundquist, *Dynamics of the Party System*, p. 351.

5. I am most grateful to the following undergraduates at the University of Michigan who collected these data: Carolyn Bradley, Debra Den Houter, Sally Everhard, Francis Gilbert, John Heidt, John Huget, Joseph Parke, Frank Raiford, Mark Tompkins, Nathaniel Warshay, and Becky Weinreich.

6. As each of the magazines contained so much less material because of its weekly rather than daily format, I have combined data from all three in order to have a large enough sample of articles to work with.

7. In part, this trend may be attributable to the decline in the sheer number of campaign-related stories per year. However, all coders were agreed that the length of the average story increased over time as the print medium struggled to compete with television by presenting the sort of in-depth coverage that television is generally not capable of. It is therefore

difficult to judge, without going through the arduous task of counting column inches, whether the amount of election coverage in fact decreased substantially. The sense of the coders was that there was somewhat less material to code over time, but certainly not to the degree necessary to account for the trend displayed in Figure 6.3.

8. I wish to thank Michael Traugott and Edie Goldenberg for kindly making these data available to me.

9. Donald E. Stokes and Warren E. Miller, "Party Government and the Saliency of Congress," *Public Opinion Quarterly* 26 (1962): 531–546.

10. See, for example, Edward R. Tufte, "Determinants of the Outcome of Midterm Congressional Elections," *American Political Science Review* 69 (1975): 812–826.

11. Thomas E. Mann and Raymond E. Wolfinger, "Candidates and Parties in Congressional Elections," *American Political Science Review* 74 (1980): 617–632.

12. Thomas E. Mann, *Unsafe at Any Margin* (Washington, D.C.: American Enterprise Institute, 1978), p. 3.

13. This measure is derived from the managers' estimates of the proportion of their total campaign budget allocated to "advertising/media."

14. Although these correlations have been calculated on the basis of data about only seventy-eight congressional districts, it should be kept in mind that the mass-level data from each district consists of approximately 20 interviews for a total of roughly 1,600. One could thus match the campaign managers' data to each respondent in the appropriate district and then perform the same correlations on a sample size twenty times greater. However, the theoretical focus of this chapter is to explain variance between districts rather than variance within districts. Therefore, in order to eliminate variance within districts, mean scores have been used throughout this analysis.

15. In all but a few cases where no preelection interview was obtained, this question was asked before the election. Therefore, the responses are not subject to rationalization based on the outcome of the election.

16. Samuel J. Eldersveld, *Political Parties: A Behavioral Analysis* (Chicago: Rand McNally, 1964).

17. Charles L. Clapp, *The Congressman: His Work as He Sees It* (New York: Doubleday, 1963), p. 397.

18. Michael J. Malbin, "Of Mountains and Molehills: PACs, Campaigns and Public Policy," in Michael J. Malbin, ed., *Parties, Interest Groups and Campaign Finance Laws* (Washington, D.C.: American Enterprise Institute, 1980), p. 154.

19. Doris A. Graber, *Mass Media and American Politics* (Washington, D.C.: Congressional Quarterly, Inc., 1980), p. 2.

20. Miller and Stokes, "Constituency Influence in Congress," p. 371.

7. Demographic Trends

1. Philip E. Converse, "Change in the American Electorate," in Angus Campbell and Philip E. Converse, eds., *The Human Meaning of Social Change* (New York: Russell Sage Foundation, 1972).

2. Everett Carll Ladd, Jr., and Charles D. Hadley, *Transformations of the American Party System* (New York: Norton, 1975), pp. 15–16.

3. Sorauf, *Party Politics in America*, p. 405.

4. See Warren E. Miller, "Disinterest, Disaffection, and Participation in Presidential Politics," *Political Behavior* 2 (1980): 7–32.

5. Arthur H. Miller and Warren E. Miller, "Rejoinder: Ideology in the 1972 Election," *American Political Science Review* 70 (1976): 832–849.

6. Converse and Markus, "Plus ça change."

7. For data on the changing relationship between age and level of education, see Warren E. Miller, Arthur H. Miller, and Edward J. Schneider, *The American National Election Studies Data Sourcebook, 1952–1978* (Cambridge, Mass.: Harvard University Press, 1980), p. 25.

8. T. W. Adorno et al., *The Authoritarian Personality* (New York: Harper, 1950).

9. Arthur H. Miller and Warren E. Miller, "Partisanship and Performance: 'Rational Choice in the 1976 Presidential Election" (paper presented at the annual meeting of the American Political Science Association, 1977).

10. Paul Allen Beck, "A Socialization Theory of Partisan Realignment," in Richard G. Niemi, ed., *The Politics of Future Citizens* (San Francisco: Jossey-Bass, 1974).

11. Nie, Verba, and Petrocik, *The Changing American Voter*, p. 68.

8. The Public as an Echo Chamber

1. V. O. Key, *The Responsible Electorate* (Cambridge, Mass.: Harvard University Press, 1966), p. 2.

2. APSA, "Toward a More Responsible Two-Party System: A report of the Committee on Political Parties, American Political Science Association," *American Political Science Review* 44 (1950): supplement, number 3, part 2.

3. See Evron M. Kirkpatrick, "Toward a More Responsible Party System: Political Science, Policy Science, or Pseudo-Science?" *American Political Science Review* 65 (1971): 965–990.

4. APSA, "Toward a More Responsible Two-Party System," p. 22.

5. Samuel J. Eldersveld, *Political Parties in American Society* (New York: Basic Books, 1982), p. x.

6. APSA, "Toward a More Responsible Two-Party System," p. 95.

7. Ibid., p. 94.

8. Ibid., p. 95.

9. See Paul R. Abramson and John H. Aldrich, "The Decline of Electoral Participation in America," *American Political Science Review* 76 (1982): 502–521.

10. Campbell et al., *The American Voter*, p. 78.

9. The Elections of 1984 and 1988

1. "No Endorsement," *Washington Post National Weekly Edition*, November 7–13, 1988, p. 32.

2. Remarks by Senator Bob Graham to the Democratic

Leadership Council, March 10, 1989, as reported on "The McNeil/Lehrer News Hour," Public Broadcasting System.

3. See the essays in Walter Dean Burnham, *The Current Crisis in American Politics* (New York: Oxford University Press, 1982).

4. Ibid., p. 10.

5. Martin P. Wattenberg, *The Decline of American Political Parties, 1952–1980* (Cambridge, Mass.: Harvard University Press, 1984), p. xvii.

6. Quoted in Lou Cannon, "The GOP Is Sizing Up Reagan's Coattails for a Ride to Victory," *Washington Post National Weekly Edition*, September 24, 1984, p. 11.

7. Quoted in ibid.

8. Herbert F. Weisberg, "The Electoral Kaleidoscope: Political Change in the Polarizing Election of 1984" (Paper presented at the annual meeting of the American Political Science Association, 1985), p. 7.

9. "Reagan Sees Vote as Poll on His Era," *New York Times*, November 6, 1988, p. A19.

10. Seymour Martin Lipset, "The U.S. Elections: The Status Quo Reaffirmed." *International Journal of Public Opinion Research* 1 (1989): 25–44.

11. Nelson W. Polsby, *Consequences of Party Reform* (New York: Oxford University Press, 1983), pp. 85–86.

12. Larry McCarthy, "The Selling of the President: An Interview with Roger Ailes," *Gannet Center Journal* 2 (Fall 1988): 67.

13. In 1960 respondents were asked which party would do better on each of up to three problems they mentioned. Unlike in 1988, they were not asked which of these problems was most important to them. To make the data as comparable as possible, I have used only responses to the first problem mentioned in 1960.

14. This contrast may stem in part from the fact that when asked about which candidate would do better, the phrase "or wouldn't there be any difference between them" was not included. This response should have been readily accepted

by the interviewers, though, given that it was one of the boxes printed on the interview schedule for them to check off. In any case, it is hardly likely that the great gap between the party and candidate responses could be accounted for by this minor difference in question wording.

15. W. Lance Bennett, *News: The Politics of Illusion*, 2d ed. (New York: Longman, 1988), p. 121.

16. Quoted in ibid., p. 123.

17. Quoted in Albert Scardino, "Choice of Most Papers Is for None of the Above," *New York Times*, November 4, 1988, p. A12.

18. See David Halberstram, *The Powers That Be* (New York: Dell Books, 1979).

19. Reuven Frank, "Let's Put On a Convention," *Gannett Center Journal* 2 (Fall 1988): 18.

20. Byron E. Shafer, *Bifurcated Politics: Evolution and Reform in the National Party Convention* (Cambridge, Mass.: Harvard University Press, 1988), p. 280.

21. For a proposal to restore a meaningful role to the convention see Martin P. Wattenberg, "When You Can't Beat Them, Join Them: Shaping the Presidential Nominating Process to the Television Age," *Polity* 21 (1989): 587–597.

22. See John E. Stanga and James F. Sheffield, "The Myth of Zero Partisanship: Attitudes toward American Political Parties, 1964–1984," *American Journal of Political Science* 31 (1987): 836.

23. Stephen C. Craig, "The Decline of Partisanship in the United States: A Reexamination of the Neutrality Hypothesis," *Political Behavior* 7 (1985): 66.

24. John G. Geer, "What Do Open-Ended Questions Measure?" *Public Opinion Quarterly* 52 (1988): 368.

25. See Martin P. Wattenberg, "The Reagan Polarization Phenomenon and the Continuing Downward Slide in Presidential Candidate Popularity," *American Politics Quarterly* 14 (1986): 219–245.

26. Larry J. Sabato, *The Party's Just Begun: Shaping Polit-*

ical Parties for America's Future (Glenview, Ill.: Scott, Foresman, 1988), p. 133.

27. David S. Broder, "No Hands Government," *Washington Post National Weekly Edition,* January 9–15, 1989, p. 4.

28. See Paul S. Herrnson, *Party Campaigning in the 1980s* (Cambridge, Mass.: Harvard University Press, 1988).

29. Joseph A. Schlesinger, "The New American Political Party," *American Political Science Review* 79 (1985): 1152–1169.

10. The 1992 Election

1. Of the National Election Study respondents who gave a reason for not voting for Perot, 31 percent mentioned his dropping out of the race in July.

2. See Bruce E. Keith, David B. Magleby, Candice J. Nelson, Elizabeth Orr, Mark C. Westlye, and Raymond E. Wolfinger, *The Myth of the Independent Voter* (Berkeley: University of California Press, 1992), p. 203.

3. Norman Ornstein and Anthony King, back cover endorsements for Keith et al., *Myth of the Independent Voter.*

4. Jacob Weisberg, "David Butler: Watching the Election with an Expert Who Knows from Truman," *Los Angeles Times,* November 1, 1992, p. M5.

5. Huffington won the seat for the Republicans by 52 to 35 percent over Ochoa, the Democratic candidate. Interestingly, the Libertarian candidate won 10 percent of the vote while spending only $18,000.

6. David S. Broder, "Clinton's No Kennedy, Either," *Washington Post National Weekly Edition,* October 12–18, p. 4.

7. For congressional years, the low point came in 1978, when only 60 percent identified with either the Democrats or the Republicans.

8. Hedrick Smith, *The Power Game: How Washington Works* (New York: Random House, 1988), p. 671.

9. Keith et al., *Myth of the Independent Voter,* p. 4.

10. Larry J. Sabato, *The Party's Just Begun: Shaping Political Parties for America's Future* (Glenview, Ill.: Scott, Foresman, 1988), p. 117.

11. Keith et al., *Myth of the Independent Voter,* p. xv.

12. Warren E. Miller, "Party Identification, Realignment, and Party Voting: Back to the Basics," *American Political Science Review* 85 (1991): 565.

13. Comparing feeling thermometer ratings of Bush and Clinton, a simulated two-party vote variable can be created for the Perot voters. Comparing these results to the congressional vote, it is found that 36 percent of the Perot voters would have split their ticket between President and House if Perot had not run.

14. Paul Allen Beck et al., "Patterns and Sources of Ticket-Splitting in Subpresidential Voting," *American Political Science Review* 86 (1992): 916–928.

15. See Philip E. Converse and Gregory B. Markus, "Plus ça change . . . The New CPS Election Study Panel," *American Political Science Review* 73 (1979): 32–49; and M. Kent Jennings and Gregory B. Markus, "Partisan Orientations over the Long Haul: Results from the Three-Wave Political Socialization Study," *American Political Science Review* 78 (1984): 1000–1018.

16. In 1992, the number seeing an important difference in what the parties stood for was 60 percent—roughly the same as it was throughout the 1980s (see Figure 9.2).

17. The election-day exit poll is used here rather than the National Election Study for two reasons. First, the exit poll contains far more interviews, and thus permits more reliable estimations of the voting behavior of various subgroups. Second, the National Election Study is substantially off the mark in terms of the vote for Clinton and Bush, though it is within one percentage point on the Perot vote.

18. The National Election Study data show only 2 percent of all African Americans voting for Perot, though with only 176 respondents this result is far less reliable than that

of the exit poll.

19. Keith et al., *Myth of the Independent Voter,* p. 167.

20. For a critique of the utility of this question see Everett Carll Ladd, "The 1992 U.S. National Election," *International Journal of Public Opinion Research* 5 (Spring 1993): 13.

21. Among Perot voters, 44 percent preferred Bush, 40 percent preferred Clinton, and 16 percent had no preference; Anderson voters split 54 percent for Carter, 33 percent for Reagan, and 13 percent no preference; 58 percent of Wallace voters preferred Nixon compared to 18 percent for Humphrey, and 24 percent no preference.

22. Edward J. Rollins, "Perot Deserves No Second Chance," *New York Times,* September 28, 1992, p. A15.

23. See Philip E. Converse and Georges Dupeux, "Politicalization of the Electorate in France and the United States," in Angus Campbell et al., *Elections and the Political Order* (New York: Wiley, 1966), pp. 269–291.

24. Theodore J. Lowi, "Mr. Perot, Form a Party; Don't Run as an Independent," *New York Times,* April 6, 1992, p. A10. See also his "The Party Crasher," *New York Times Magazine,* August 23, 1992, pp. 28, 33.

25. Theodore J. Lowi, "The Dog That Did Not Bark: Ross Perot and the Prospects for a Permanent Third Party," *Extensions* (Spring 1993): 11.

26. Andrew Rosenthal, "Quayle Says Perot Displays Contempt for Constitution," *New York Times,* June 13, 1992, p. A1.

27. Helen Dewar, "The Politics of Gridlock," *Washington Post National Weekly Edition,* August 10–16, 1992, p. 6.

28. Morris P. Fiorina, *Divided Government* (New York: MacMillan, 1992), p. 3.

29. Morris P. Fiorina, "The Reagan Years: Turning to the Right or Groping toward the Middle?" in Barry Cooper et al., eds., *The Resurgence of Conservatism in Anglo-American Democracies* (Durham, N.C.: Duke University Press, 1988), p. 442.

30. See the data reported in *The Public Perspective* (January/February 1993): 107–108.

31. Voting for Perot was unrelated to the question of unified or divided party control of the two elected branches.

32. Gary C. Jacobson, *The Electoral Origins of Divided Government: Competition in U.S. House Elections, 1946–1988* (Boulder, Colo.: Westview Press, 1990), p. 106.

33. John R. Petrocik, "Divided Government: Is It All in the Campaigns?" in Gary W. Cox and Samuel Kernell, *The Politics of Divided Government* (Boulder, Colo.: Westview Press, 1991), pp. 13–38. For a similar argument, see Byron E. Shafer, "The Notion of an Electoral Order: The Structure of Electoral Politics at the Accession of George Bush," in Byron E. Shafer, ed., *The End of Realignment? Interpreting American Electoral Eras* (Madison, Wis.: University of Wisconsin Press, 1991), pp. 37–84.

34. Fiorina, *Divided Government,* p. 45.

35. See Jacobson, *The Electoral Origins of Divided Government.*

36. See Alan Ehrenhalt, *The United States of Ambition: Politicians, Power, and the Pursuit of Office* (New York: Random House, 1991).

37. See Martin P. Wattenberg, *The Rise of Candidate-Centered Politics: Presidential Elections of the 1980s* (Cambridge, Mass.: Harvard University Press, 1991), chap. 3.

38. See Elaine Ciulla Kamarck, "Structure as Strategy: Presidential Nominating Politics in the Post-Reform Era," in L. Sandy Maisel, ed., *The Parties Respond: Changes in the American Party System* (Boulder, Colo.: Westview Press), pp. 160–186.

39. Figure 9.1 shows how realignment in the 1980s made it possible for the Republicans to win by focusing more on just their own voters. In 1992 the GOP took this too far, with 83 percent of Bush's votes coming from Republican identifiers or Independent Republicans. The result was a coalition too narrow for a presidential election victory.

40. Robert Shogan, "Clinton's Last Hurdle Gone, Experts

Say," *Los Angeles Times,* March 20, 1992, p. A1.

41. See David R. Mayhew, *Divided We Govern: Party Control, Lawmaking, and Investigations, 1946–1990* (New Haven: Yale University Press, 1991).

42. James L. Sundquist, *Constitutional Reform and Effective Government,* rev. ed. (Washington, D.C.: Brookings Institution, 1992), p. 105.

Index